CHURCH FAMILY MINISTRY

CHURCH FAMILY MINISTRY

changing loneliness to fellowship in the church

Susan B. Lidums
Foreword by
Ronald W. Brusius

Publishing House
St. Louis

3558 S. Jefferson Avenue, St. Louis, MO 63118-3968
Manufactured in the United States of America

Library of Congress Cataloging in Publication Data

Lidums, Susan B., 1944–
Church-family ministry

1. Church work with families. 2. Pastoral theology.
I. Title.
BV4438.L53 1985 259 84-15590
ISBN 0-570-03945-2

---

1 2 3 4 5 6 7 8 9 10 MAL 94 93 92 91 90 89 88 87 86 85

To Olaf,
partner in family and
co-worker in family ministry.

Contents

Foreword

How to do family ministry in the church evokes many different responses from church professionals and lay people. Parish pastors are all too familiar with the complaint that there are not enough family programs, marriage programs, youth programs, or singles programs in the congregation.

A regional church official, charged with coordinating a multitude of programs—including family life education—once remarked that family life ministries were the hardest to "get a handle on." His words are not unfamiliar to anybody who has seriously attempted family ministries in more than a haphazard way that simply reacts to the urgent cry of the moment.

There are several reasons for the lack of a "handle." Most training programs for church professionals give no more attention than a quick brush stroke to the area of family life education. Most are more concerned with providing help for families and individuals in crisis than with strengthening families and individuals so that they are able to effectively face the day-to-day concerns of life and weather the extraordinary events that will confront any family in its journey through the life cycle.

Yet another reason for the hazy focus in family ministries lies in defining the family as two parents and their children and then trying to equate that family with the church family. Many individuals and families feel excluded from congregational offerings because they believe that they are directed at that two-parents-and-their-children family.

At the same time the church is the one institution in society that touches people at all of the significant stages in the life cycle—from birth to death and all of the touchstones in between. Often church people don't recognize the contact that they do have with people apart from Sunday morning worship, and thus they neglect opportunities for taking advantage of "teaching moments" in the lives of the parish members and others who seek the services of the church.

Often too, churches try to compete with community organizations and forget that the central mission is to minister with individuals and units so that they may live fuller lives in Jesus Christ, who came that we may have life—eternally, yes, but also more abundantly now.

Church-Family Ministry is a book that all persons who touch the lives of others in congregational ministries should read because it broadens the perspective of what ministry to families and individuals is and puts the ideas in manageable and readable terms.

The author starts with a look at the church of her childhood, which still exists in some areas, and moves to the church of her children, which is a much more common type. The church of today has changed just as the society has changed. Family growth, which happened almost routinely in the past, is not routine today.

Each congregation needs to look intentionally at what it does to strengthen individuals and families. *Church-Family Ministry* will aid in taking that look in an easy, systematic way.

One of the services that the book provides is its emphasis on wellness—a concept familiar to many and probably foreign to just as many. The model previously used was based on illness and had as its purpose to help people recover from illness or keep from getting sick. Today's model, which appears to be more Scriptural, is shifting the emphasis to wellness so that people take full advantage of who they are in Jesus Christ as forgiven sinners and who they can be because of what Christ makes possible.

If the ideas of this book are new to you, read it yourself first, and then discuss it with other people who have congregational ministry responsibilities. Implementing the step-by-step suggestions contained in this book will help you to "get a handle on" the task of ministry with individuals and families in the church.

RONALD W. BRUSIUS
Secretary of Family Life Education
Board for Parish Services
Lutheran Church—Missouri Synod

Introduction

Having grown up in the fellowship of a rural Wisconsin church, I suspect ministry to families has long been a part of church tradition. Out of that church came my godparents, who to this day remember me with gifts of faith. When I shyly dangled my feet from a little red cradle-roll chair, stretching to touch toe with the floor, it was my grandmother who planted my lifelong memory of Bible characters in her cake-pan sandbox. Each Sunday every pew was filled with familiar faces who greeted my grandparents, my parents, and even my siblings and me by name. By the time I was eight, they knew my voice and listened with tender support to our sister trio sing in trembling voice "Were You There?"

That church gave me my first job, clipping the grass around each tombstone on the hills of its five-acre cemetery, and that church responded to the economic needs of my family when our barn burned a year later.

I am still recognized and respected when I return to that community of faith, though few of my relatives remain on their membership list. Its generations still nurture me as I wander through the cemetery.

I suspect that the church is rich in a tradition of ministry to families.

All of that seemed to need no intentional structure or attention. Ministry to families happened—or didn't happen—through informal response to neighbors and relatives we knew. No programs for intentional care or support set up the food deliveries in crises; no prayer chains were typed on some office list or in some file box on some desk; no talent or need or interest surveys were circulated. Perhaps much was neglected—probably no more than gets overlooked in any organized file. I certainly recall a sad lack of young adult programs and talk of unsatisfied needs, but because the church was an extended family for so many (many of them in blood lines), ministry to family at all ages and in all needs somehow happened informally. And intergenerational events were a natural part of church activities: The Nativity pageant was as much an event for the adults as for the scrubbed and glowing youth; the spring Sunday school picnic was a chance for the men to play softball too; and church cleaning seemed ample excuse for a potluck.

I have belonged to seven congregations since I left that community. My children see no relatives in the pews, often even no neighbors. When we adopted our second child, most didn't notice the event. When my husband spent two weeks in the hospital for major back surgery, only the pastor knew of it. Certainly none knew of crises in our marriage, painful struggles as parents, or anxieties of mid-life. Yet I am a regular member of a friendly church, a church dedicated to ministry to others, to education at all ages, and to "sharing the peace" in warm handclasp with each other.

Many share my experience.

Congregations across the country are noting an increase in mobility, an increase in families with no natural ties, an increase in isolated individuals and isolated family units. Indeed, how can we respond to a need we never noticed in people we never knew?

Another social change has happened. Church often used to be the center of community activities. The young learned sportsmanship from playing softball in church leagues as much as on the school grounds. Hayrides and skating parties were more often church events than class parties. Even my husband, who spent his youth in Chicago, remembers learning to dance in church basements. Public schools now fill the hours of the young with athletic meets and extracurricular activities. The secular community entertains our young and often ties up our adults in voluntarism and community action. The church is no longer the natural center of social activity for most of its members. Many churches report that well-planned youth events are unattended; choirs dissolve because fewer and fewer find time to commit; Sunday school classes fold because of erratic attendance and lack of teachers; and vacation Bible school doors never open because no one registers. The only sure regular family event in many churches is Sunday worship, and even that suffers in the throes of summer.

Yet lay people are voicing a need for meaningful involvement in the church and are asking that the church minister to their families in a time when many feel the stress of economic and social pressures and are anxious about rapid social changes and demands. Is what we are offering superfluous? . . . insignificant? . . . unimportant?

. . . irrelevant? I doubt it. The programs of many congregations are solid, well-staffed, interesting, and highly commendable. At issue is rather what is *not* being offered. Ministry to families is particularly piecemeal. Caring, holistic ministry, ministry that is sensitive to total family units and to all the interrelated facets of each person in Christ, might be lacking—a ministry that once happened quite informally and now requires an intentional vision.

Developing a holistic ministry to families need not mean adding programs to already overcrowded church schedules. It need not mean throwing out programs that are already effective. It does mean building a comprehensive program that brings people of all ages together, intentionally ministering in each person's individual circumstance and stage in life. Simply stated, it means the church may again "be with" each from birth to death in supportive, caring ministry in the family.

For those congregations, clergy, and lay people who wish to explore such ministry, I share this practical vision of intentional ministry to families.

1. Who Is Family?

The first thing that needs to change is our picture of the family. The image of the family as two parents living together with two or more children under their roof is far from the norm. Current estimates suggest that no more than 33 percent of American families fit that mold. Over half of that 33 percent are two-income families. Since full-time working women do not always fit comfortably into everyone's traditional image, our estimate is down to nearly 11 percent or even lower. Single-parent families, with a continual increase in men as heads of those households, account for as much as 30 percent of American families. Many of the remaining third are single-person households—single young adults; retired singles, many of whom are widows; and an increasing number who are singles by choice. When we talk of ministry to families, can we limit our view to less than a third of our families?

In practical sociological terms, family seems to mean household. In more important emotional terms, families are primary caring and nurturing units of people living together by choice or by birth. Families so defined come in a multitude of shapes and forms. "Family" includes single-parent families, blended families, adoptive families, units of adults joined for care and support, childless couples—and the list goes on to include all who are in committed relationship to others. Families, in popular terms, are people who share their daily lives together, most often under the same roof—which means that for the most part we all live in families. To live in close relationship with others is to live in a family. We need to become more inclusive in our definition of family and to recognize that family in its many forms is most simply our primary unit of nurture and care.

Although we may understandably regret the loss of structures that were dear to us, this need not be a frustrating picture to us in the Christian tradition.

In Biblical history families were as diverse as they are today. The shape each took had much to do with time and location. Nomadic tribes consisted of households of male leaders and their many wives, children, servants, and cattle. Some of Abraham's descendants were born not of his wife but of the maidservant Hagar. We teach our children the story of Jacob, who worked diligently to earn two wives. The tribes of Israel lived in family clans. Surely Ruth in her loyalty felt closest kin to her mother-in-law. Her oath of commitment to Naomi remains a model expression of the meaning of family in a wedding pledge today. Samuel, from his mother's early vow of thankfulness to God, found his family as much in the tabernacle in the presence of Yahweh and the priests as with his devoted mother. And this, too, is a treasured Sunday school story, not a tale of child neglect.

Little mention is made of the families of the prophets; what seemed to matter was that they were most clearly of the household of God. And perhaps most radically, Jesus called his disciples from their fathers and mothers to be brothers and sisters in a new community. From that time on we were all to be brothers and sisters in Christ. In Scripture family took its many forms from social times and practical needs, and most significantly, it took the form and shape needed to fulfill God's purpose.

With a tradition so pluralistic I would hate to see us omit any in God's household when we sit down to determine who is "family" in our midst!

Yet these are merely some of the forms of family found in Scripture. The Biblical vision of family is much broader. In Hebrew the word signifying "family" is an action word, a verb, and thus cannot simply define a static form. How, then, does family happen in Scripture?

The most comprehensive image of family in the Bible is all of God's creation as family. Family happens by God's act of creation. A number of Psalms celebrate the unity of all of creation.

> The earth is the Lord's and the fullness thereof,
> the world and those who dwell therein;
> for He has founded it upon the seas,
> and established it upon the rivers. (Ps. 24:1-2)

All creation is within the realm of God's family of creation and awaits eagerly its fulfillment.

> For the creation waits with eager longing for the revealing of the sons of God; for the creation was subjected to futility, not of its

> own will but by the will of Him who subjected it in hope; because the creation itself will be set free from its bondage to decay and obtain the glorious liberty of the children of God. We know that the whole creation has been groaning in travail together until now. (Romans 8:19-22)

There is an implied familial unity within all creation.

Family happens in God's act of making covenant. In redemptive promise God established a covenant with Noah and his sons, a covenant that included every living creature and every living thing. By God's act of making covenant, all creation is the family of God. With every rainbow we are reminded:

> This is the sign of the covenant which I make between Me and you and every living creature that is with you, for all future generations: I set My bow in the cloud, and it shall be a sign of the covenant between Me and the earth. When I bring clouds over the earth and the bow is seen in the clouds, I will remember My covenant which is between Me and you and every living creature of all flesh; and the waters shall never again become a flood to destroy all flesh. When the bow is in the clouds, I will look upon it and remember the everlasting covenant between God and every living creature of all flesh that is upon the earth. (Gen. 9:12-16)

Lying in the summer grass, fingernails deep in sand and soil, my young children sense that unity better than I. And when my son shares his exciting discovery that he has a special language with the family dog, I am humbly aware that I am not a part of that intimate secret. Sometimes all I know of this familial unity with creation is its disharmonious absence as I struggle with gardening neglected soil, battling slugs and bugs in my jealous possession of one small plot of land. It takes greater distance and a panoramic view for me to arrive at this broadest Biblical view of family. But to this vision we need to call our families.

Another basic view of family found in Scripture is that all people who roam the earth are kin to each other and to God. In Isaiah we see the prophetic vision of the Lord preparing a banquet "for all peoples" (Is. 25:6). Isaiah's vision of the Lord freeing his people reaches to all corners of the earth:

> I will say to the north, Give up,
> and to the south, Do not withhold;
> bring My sons from afar
> and My daughters from the end of the earth,

everyone who is called by My name,
whom I created for My glory,
whom I formed and made. (Is. 43:6-7)

It is not strangers but God's created people, descendants of Noah, who were scattered "over the face of all the earth" at the time of Babel (Gen. 11).

This view of family certainly challenges us to wake up to the presence and needs of the children of the third world, for they too are our brothers and sisters. I mention this not as a sideline but as a central image we need to keep alive among families within our own home congregations. Biblically, all people of all races and times are created children of God.

Perhaps the most central image of family in Scripture is the people of God, bearing God's name, fulfilling God's purpose, and living within the blessing of God's household.

In the Old Testament this is the family of Israel. In a national song of praise, the psalmist triumphantly celebrates:

> Rain in abundance, O God, Thou didst shed abroad;
> Thou didst restore Thy heritage as it languished;
> Thy flock found a dwelling in it;
> in Thy goodness, O God, Thou didst provide for the needy.
> (Ps. 68:9-10)
>
> The God of Israel . . . gives power and strength to His people.
> (v. 35)

God is honored as the "Father of the fatherless" (v. 5), a God who "gives the desolate a home to dwell in" (v. 6).

And when Solomon establishes the ark in the temple and addresses the assembly, he praises the "God of Israel" who brought His people Israel "out of the land of Egypt" (1 Kings 8:14, 21). From within the temple Solomon prays:

> When Thy people Israel are defeated before the enemy because they have sinned against Thee, if they turn again to Thee, and acknowledge Thy name, and pray and make supplication to Thee in this house; then hear Thou in heaven, and forgive the sin of Thy people Israel, and bring them again to the land which Thou gavest to their fathers. (1 Kings 8:33-34)

The Old Testament story of God's chosen people is a story of a family whose purpose it is to be the people of God.

As the people of God, Israel is to remain loyal to Yahweh and instruct her children in the way:

> Hear, O Israel: The Lord our God is one Lord; and you shall love the Lord your God with all your heart, and with all your soul, and with all your might. And these words which I command you this day shall be upon your heart; and you shall teach them diligently to your children, and shall talk of them when you sit in your house, and when you walk by the way, and when you lie down, and when you rise. (Deut. 6:4-7)

The family transcends generations; it is a people of history and promise.

The concept of the people of God in the New Testament expands from Israel to include all who bear God's name. The author of 1 John marvels: "See what love the Father has given us, that we should be called children of God; and so we are" (1 John 3:1). Paul in his letter to the Romans writes:

> For all who are led by the Spirit of God are sons of God. For you did not receive the spirit of slavery to fall back into fear, but you have received the spirit of sonship. When we cry, "Abba! Father!" it is the Spirit Himself bearing witness with our spirit that we are children of God, and if children, then heirs, heirs of God and fellow heirs with Christ, provided we suffer with Him in order that we may also be glorified with Him. (Romans 8:14-17)

This enriched image of the people of God—a family in Christ—came out of the tradition of Christ's teaching. Jesus brought disciples together in new family unity and purpose. Indeed, when His relatives sought to have a word with Him, Jesus replied, "Who is My mother, and who are My brothers?" Then He pointed toward His disciples and said, "Here are My mother and brothers! For whoever does the will of My Father in heaven is My brother, and sister, and mother" (Matt. 12:48-50).

This New Testament image of family as the people of God is further developed in the image of the body of Christ with Christ as its head: "Now you are the body of Christ" (1 Cor. 12:27). And for what purpose?

> Put on then, as God's chosen ones, holy and beloved, compassion, kindness, lowliness, meekness, and patience, forbearing one another and, if one has a complaint against another, forgiving each other; as the Lord has forgiven you, so you also must forgive. And above all these put on love, which binds everything together in perfect harmony. And let the peace of Christ rule in your hearts, to which indeed you were called in the one body. And be thankful.

> Let the word of Christ dwell in you richly, teach and admonish one another in all wisdom, and sing psalms and hymns and spiritual songs with thankfulness in your hearts to God. And whatever you do, in word or deed, do everything in the name of the Lord Jesus, giving thanks to God the Father through Him. (Col. 3:12-17)

All who bear God's name participate in this image of family—brothers and sisters in Christ.

The definition of family as a small household unit is but one of four images of family in the Scriptures, and it always fits within the broader definition of what it means to be the people of God, children of God, and part of God's creation.

Teachings on life in the primary family are always in this broader context. Husbands and wives are admonished to "be subject to one another out of reverence to Christ" (Eph. 5:21). Children are to obey in accord with God's plan and promise:

> "Honor your father and mother" (this is the first commandment with a promise), "that it may be well with you and that you may live long on the earth." (Eph. 6:2-3)

In turn, parents are not to anger their children but "bring them up in the discipline and instruction of the Lord" (v. 4).

Family households are a part of the larger community and purpose. Mary and Joseph must certainly have been aware of this in their journey to Bethlehem, in their messenger-guided flight into Egypt, and in their very upbringing of Jesus. If not, Jesus Himself certainly reminded them at an early age that He must be about His Father's business (Luke 2:41-50). Biblical households are a part of a larger family of God, but they are certainly not all the same, as noted earlier. Small household units in the New Testament are quite different from those in the Old Testament, and within each Testament there is a wide variety of structure and form.

So when we speak of ministry to families, we need a vision of family that includes all people in committed relationship to others and to all of God's creation.

I admit that I was quite taken aback when a single, 50-year-old farmer showed up at a family workshop a few years back. What surprised me more was to watch him discover in one of the activities that he had little to put into a circle that was drawn around things he did alone. His larger concentric circle, representing life shared with others, was filled beyond the perimeters, and it was obvious from the delight of those at his table that they were his family. I understood then why he had not excluded himself from a study of life together in family.

Not long ago a lay leader asked my advice on how to tell a 60-year-old single woman that she perhaps did not belong in a family workshop series we had planned. Recalling the farmer, I suggested we let her decide that for herself—and indeed she did. She came to a better understanding of her family relationship with dozens of developmentally retarded children for whom she is foster grandmother.

Octogenarian siblings who have spent a lifetime together in family contributed to another workshop I will never forget simply because of their involved and delighted presence. And one of the closest family units I recall was a family of two parents, their two teenaged children, and a menagerie of teens who felt at home in their midst.

Including all varieties and forms of families in family ministry and activities within our congregations is exciting and essential. A more narrow vision of family would deny the whole essence of what it means to be together in primary caring and nurturing relationship. The single-parent family is a system of nurturing care just as much as the two-parent family of four. The multigenerational family, the childless couple, the "blended" or "step-family"—all experience the same basic dynamics of love and sharing in family tasks.

In developing a church-family ministry, we need a vision of family that includes all who see themselves struggling and delighting in meaningful relationship with others.

2. Why Is Ministry to Family So Important?

That families are in need of support and care is perhaps obvious. Those who work in counseling and family therapy note that there seems to be an increase in what are clinically called "disfunctional families," that is, families who are not able to function as a relatively healthy family. In extremes, this shows up in an increase of reported incest and abuse, an increase in violence in the home, and a high increase in "problem youth."

The statistics merely validate what we notice and experience in our own neighborhoods. The divorce rate almost doubled from 1968 to 1978 and continues to rise. A conservative estimate is that by 1990 half of all children in America will have lived in single-parent households during some time in their childhood. With the increase of women in the job market, day care is replacing much home care for preschoolers, and "latch-key children" (children carrying house keys to let themselves into empty houses at the end of the day) fill the public classrooms. These statistics reveal the disintegrating forces and pressures that most families are under.

We all know neighbors and parishioners who have divorced; many of us have "gone through" at least one divorce—our own or that of a close friend, our parents, or our children. We have worked with, carpooled, or lived with children from single-parent households, and we may know the fatigue and stress of their parents. I watch the delivery of child-care toddlers from my kitchen window—over half a dozen on our block alone—delivered before most of my household is even awake and picked up well after daylight wanes. I have fed many of those "latch-key" children with house keys around their necks and watched them track through my home. Some of the more forlorn need prodding to head home to empty houses. The phenomenon is so widespread that it is like a fad; my children sometimes beg to be a part of it simply to feel important and in style. There is pain and frustration behind the statistics, pain we have all seen and known.

When I recently taught school full-time again, I found that I had to put my primary relationship with my husband "on the back burner." There wasn't enough time or energy to go around in a family of four. Everything was somehow tended to—we ate; we wore clean clothes; the house was never quite a total disaster area; the children got to sports events and music lessons; we went to church and Sunday school; we kept up with the household records and major repairs; we even celebrated birthdays. The children were not truly neglected and learned some good things about pitching in around the home and about appreciating Mom as someone other than "mother." But our emotional and spiritual needs were not met; none of us felt nurtured—or nurturing. We felt organized, efficient, capable—but not always particularly lovable. Family nurturing takes time, energy, and attention that we did not have. Worse yet, without support or deliberate awareness, we gave it so little time or energy.

If I experience such stress in a two-parent family, imagine the predicament of the single parent. The parent of preschoolers is alone in facing the frustration of overwork and coping with the constant demands of young children. The single parent of teens, again alone, faces not only the typical stress of life with teens but also the dilemma of authority—having to depend on teens as partners in family responsibility and yet recognize that they still need to be supervised and guided. On top of that, single parents may struggle with feelings left over from the loss or separation that got them into the single experience—the feelings of loneliness and the reshaping of personal identity. Economic need often places the single parent in the situation of having to take any job simply to provide for the family. And for many there is ongoing tension with the other parent who, though absent, is still parent to the children.

Economic necessity or circumstances put many of us in equally demanding work or family predicaments. Is it any wonder that there is so much depression, anxiety, stress-related illness, drug and alcohol abuse, "breaking out," and "acting out" in our families?

If current popular literature and statistics are correct, most of us are in our predicaments alone. We are disconnected from our natural family ties, having moved away from our hometown or set up our own households. Most of us have no support system. We don't dare ask too much of our neighbors; we may not even know them. We might find friends here or there who will listen or trade help and support, but they seem to come and go. We may find a few people with whom we would feel comfortable sharing family concerns, but they are usually too near our own age to have the experience or wisdom we would hope for, and they often are tied up with concerns of their own. Our adolescents have no other parent figures to turn to. The only marriage we have ever really known is our own. We may never have experienced, seen, or even heard of an outrageous tantrum of a three-year-old or the sassy indignance of an early teen.

The isolation most families experience increases the pressure. We are expected to maintain a household, raise responsible and healthy children, be good partners to each other in marriage, provide a good home for all within it, see that each family member has an opportunity to grow and to learn, tend to our physical and emotional health, model and pass on ethical behavior and treasured values—all this and more *by ourselves.*

Housing trends of the past decade have led us into some of this isolation and have at the same time increased demands on us economically and socially. The shift from single-family dwellings to apartments that mushroomed in the seventies brought about a shift in our relationship to our physical and social environment. These dwellings were not ours to own or even to choose to lease for a lifetime. We began to see less commitment to the dwelling and to the neighbors, perhaps even to each other within the family. Moving became easier and happened more frequently.

Initially, moving into an apartment often meant moving away from family or out of a neighborhood we may have known for most of our life. As individuals and as small family units we were uprooted from tradition and place. Apartments, though often more convenient, were also less private. Now others could overhear much of our private life—and those others were neither family nor friends but simply someone who happened to live next door. Isolation within close proximity to others is most difficult. The shift to apartments made it harder to create a distinctive homey environment in the sameness of economy dwellings. Without this self-expression, we can begin to lose a sense of family identity and tradition.

Another trend emerged in apartment living: buildings were set aside for particular types of people. "No Children" and "No Pets" became common restrictions. Couples who had settled into an apartment were forced to locate new housing as they chose to begin a family. This meant that they had to begin their new life as parents in the isolation of a whole new community. It also meant that whole communities developed for singles, for the elderly, and for small families—often designed as such, but sometimes simply resulting from the fact that they were one-bedroom apartment buildings. Although this brought people of similar life circumstance together, it separated whole groups from cross-sectional relationships, from other ethnic traditions, and from a broader sense of community. We are just beginning to look at the long-range psychological effects of such segregation as whole states like Florida find themselves consisting predominantly of one age group.

The rise in popularity of condominiums has also added stress to some families and to whole communities. Besides involving a major shift in type of housing that is perhaps too recent for us to comprehend in terms of its social significance, condominiums are not so affordable. For many, the conversion of an apartment to a condominium means an inevitable move. Most make this move in a matter of months, but where do they move? They may have to leave their established neighborhood. Whole neighborhoods, particularly stable, low-income neighborhoods, can be rejuggled or relocated in the wake of a major condominium project.

These trends, along with a present shortage in housing in many large American cities, add to the stress and isolation of our present life. It may not be inevitable that they continue to do so. If we meet the challenges of living closer together, of mobility, and of cooperative housing, we may discover new forms of community that provide fellowship and support. But for now we need to recognize that these trends have created needs to be addressed.

The milieu of our society also adds to the pressures we all experience. Exciting advertising makes it hard for us to know or remember our own priorities. Bombarded by enticements for what others call necessities, we get caught up in consumerism. On top of that, "youth" is inordinately glamorized. It is hard for my young daughter to believe that it is truly all right to be 39 when she has spent most of her years dreaming of life as a teenager, caught up in a world of Barbies and teenage "pop." We are told by the media that we must be beautiful. When we pass our teens, we must pay to stay at least youthful in style. Sex is blasted at us from the media as merely a recreational pleasure, not a pleasure of the marriage relationship. We're confused because "Do your own thing!" is the overt slogan of America. Yet we are pressured to conform. And we are measured by our worth on the job, by what we can earn, and particularly by our productivity—and more is always expected. The rapidity of social change alone is enough to confuse and frustrate us.

For all of these reasons, families need support and ministry. All families experience frustrations, pressures, and anxieties, some more than others. The need for support and ministry is there; is it up to the church to respond?

Response to families in need is nothing new for the church. But maybe "need" has been too narrowly defined as "crisis." One of the first questions that comes up in exploring marriage enrichment within congregations is, Do we have enough marriages that need help? Couples are actually afraid to sign up for fear others will think they are having serious problems. Perhaps if we broaden our definition of need, a response would be quite natural. We all need ministry, which is the active caring Word of God in our lives. In continued response to families in need within our congregations and in our communities, our mission is to ask, What is the need? not, Is your family in need?

Understandably, the church does not choose to respond to all needs in society, and perhaps rightly so. Schools are seen as better equipped to teach people to read; hospitals tend better to physical needs; treatment centers know well how to work with alcoholics. The church need not try to meet every social need. In many of these social issues the church can and does choose a supportive, not an administratively responsible, role. So why tend to the family? Are there not family institutes, counseling centers, community centers, and YMCAs to do that? Yes, they do—mostly by meeting specific needs or in a clinical way. Family needs are social needs and are therefore a concern of all of society—secular needs, as it were. But the family is also a concern of the church.

The heritage of the Christian church is rich in emphasis on the family. Apart from images already explored, family as a primary unit of structure and care was carefully supported by customs and laws in the Old Testament. Life together in primary caring and nurturing family units was the closest parallel to the relationship of God to man in Jesus' teachings. The early church, according to the New Testament, gave special attention to the quality of relationships between family members. Paul, in his letters to the Ephesians and Corinthians, said much about the obedience of children, their nurturing by parents, and the love between husband and wife. Living in family was a means of serving God and doing God's will.

Martin Luther recognized the family as a form in which God's grace was revealed. Family was a "vocation," a "calling" even beyond the calling to do well in every work in this world. Luther saw the family as one of the *larvae dei* (masks of God—forms in which God works in the world), created and instituted by God. This was particularly emphasized in the task of raising a family. He was appalled at the very idea that a man would leave his family responsibilities to join some righteous missionary expedition. His personal vocation in family was no easier or smoother than ours, as you can discover with amusement in the stories of his sometimes harsh and rigid family. If not the most fun, it was certainly one of his most serious tasks in life.

The fact that the traditional image of mother, father, and two or more children became so established in the church as the ideal model of the Christian family shows the importance that the church in more recent decades has placed on family. Such a model is obviously narrow and exclusive, but it does attest to a genuine concern for the family. Keeping the family intact is a major concern of many local congregations—and of the church body as a whole. Marriage is a religious service; divorce is not. Maintaining the structure of family is an honoring of important vows made before God in the eyes of the church. The church already has both a vested interest in and a concern for the structure of the family.

When I was in late elementary school, I was part of the transition that led to the closing of many one-room schoolhouses. Through the seventh grade I liked the sunny, open, and clean schoolroom, the competitive softball games, the elaborate Christmas programs, the well-stocked library off to the side of the room, and the secure presence of three siblings. I liked the "open classroom" freedom I found there. I learned a lot. And I remember the strong community concern to keep that structure alive in the face of increasing consolidations. In the eighth grade a sudden move by our family brought me to another one-room school. Here the room was dingy with plaster that fell faster than anyone cared to sweep it. The library was one small shelf of lower-level books; even the textbooks were sorely limited. I was ashamed to tell others where I went to school. I looked the other way when we drove past its unkempt grounds. Yet I remember the same bitter controversy over closing that school, too. Can our concern as a church be limited to simply preserving structures? Is there any concern about the crumbling plaster or the quality of learning and relationships within the structure?

If we in congregations are concerned about family—a concern that has been important throughout the history of the church—then our concern needs to reach as far as the life within families. And if we take seriously the New Testament teachings of life together in Christ, we must translate that into life together in family. Social response to families in need is fundamental to the health of human society, but it will not adequately replace Christian ministry to the spirit of families. As work in the kingdom of God and in the kingdom of the world, both need our caring ministry.

Life together in family is a fundamental concern of the church. What happens in our household is a model of life together in community as we live in grace as the people of God. In family we see possibilities for the whole scope of active ministry— care, protection, food, shelter, support, love—all rich in tradition and values and done with cooperation and spiritual awareness. In truth, ministry is taught and learned in the family. If the church is the people of God in community, then the family is its primary unit. If the calling of the church is to be the people of God, then just as surely the calling and primary function of each household is likewise to be the people of God.

Paul's prayer in his letter to the Ephesians reminds us that this work of God is alive in all families:

> For this reason I bow my knees before the Father, from whom every family in heaven and on earth is named, that according to the riches of His glory He may grant you to be strengthened with might through His Spirit in the inner man, and that Christ may dwell in your hearts through faith; that you, being rooted and grounded in love, may have power to comprehend with all the saints what is the breadth and length and height and depth, and to know the love of Christ which surpasses knowledge, that you may be filled with all the fullness of God. (Eph. 3:14-19)

This vision of God at work in families is most focused in the New Testament image of the body of Christ. In Ephesians, Romans, and 1 Corinthians we read repeatedly of the need to build up the body, respecting each member's function, and to be bound together in the love of Christ. That we are to bear each other's burdens, care for each other, and live patiently, kindly, and honestly with each other is all part of our call to life in Christ. And it is also part of our daily lives in community, which is, for most of us, in family.

It seems obvious that we defeat ourselves in parish ministry when we omit family ministry. To minister effectively within and outside our congregations, we first need the foundation of nurturing, caring units—households within God's family. The strength of our households is at the core of our strength as a church. If our families are not functioning as the people of God, then we lack the foundation to be the community of Christ.

It is significant that the two sacraments of "GOD WITH US" are community and family events. Children are baptized as children of God within a family, to be raised and nurtured in the faith within congregation and family. One of our Sunday school children's impression that Baptism is the "God-baby-family-church thing" is most accurate. Maybe our church tradition has sometimes seemed to promote a highly individualistic notion of Communion, but community is at the heart of this sacrament too. The body and blood of Christ is with us in community. The Word is made flesh in family. Life together in Christ is sacramental. We are called to live in Christian love and community—to each other. This has to mean family as well as church community. So the church as the family of the households of God has a call to minister to those households.

The church lives in a covenant relationship—covenanted to God from the beginning of time, as so persistently proclaimed in the Old Testament, and covenanted to each other as the Word is made flesh and dwells among us. Family is also a covenant relationship. Covenant is not a worldly theme that warrants much secular support. It goes beyond reasonable contract and natural consequence. It rests in unconditional love, persistent and permanent commitment, and unending forgiveness and grace. We won't find this nurtured or supported in secular terms. The task of the spiritual enrichment of families is a task of the church, for the church understands covenant and lives in hope and promise of complete fullness. To believe that God is at work in all families is to believe that the church is part of that work. Families need the active support and involvement of the Christian community to live more fully in covenant with each other and with God.

The covenant nature of the family is very real to me as an adoptive parent. That moment of accepting a child into our family—unconditionally and with no physical belonging—was a moment of covenant as profound to us as was our covenant of marriage. Here was an "other," not an extension of ourselves but a separate person, who from henceforth was one of us. The symbiotic ties and bonding we were to know later with each child never replaced the importance of that original covenant. In the Sacrament of Baptism, the church became not only witness to but also part of that covenant. What might it mean for the church to live out that covenant?

Many institutions are and will continue to be educationally, recreationally, and therapeutically supportive of families. Few have the holistic potential that is possible within the church. For the church has the potential of knowing the whole family and of being with each person from birth to death. The church can be there at each life stage, in liturgy and personal presence. All dimensions and stages of life can be touched and explored in Christian community. My work, my parenting, my primary relationships, my mental and physical health, my environment, my social involvement, my talents, and my inhibitions—all these and more are within the realm of my "life in Christ." Unlike other institutions that are limited to one focus, one age, or one area, the church spans all. In truth, the church is the only institution that cares most centrally for the meaning and spirit of life that is at the center of each of us. What an exciting opportunity and mission!

At a time when so many families feel a lack of power and a sense of helplessness, an active ministry in word and deed can set them free! This is why ministry to families is such an important task of the church.

3. What Is Ministry to Family?

If there is no ideal model of family, what is the goal of our ministry to family? Toward what are we aiming?

It is not so much an aim or a goal; it is a directional leaning that is at stake. Families are complicated systems that are not simply "well" or "not well," clearly "good" or "bad," clinically "in need of help" or "not in need of help."

Think of your own family for a minute. Are there not days that start off badly from the very beginning, days of chaotic disorder, irritability, or miscommunication? Are there not also days of harmony, cooperation, and enjoyment? Where do we put ourselves on that wide spectrum of family life—"good" or "not good"? What is your honest response to, "How are you today?"—"Fine" or "Sick"? Isn't it more honestly, "I've had better days," "I'm a little anxious," "This is a good day for me," or "I think I'm coming down with something, but I'm in good spirits"? Even within ourselves we are complicated systems. Imagine the variations in a family of four—or six!

Rather than placing families into precise categories of need or behavior, it is most helpful to recognize that we live on a continuum of "wellness." At one extreme, we may feel "very sick" and in immediate, even desperate, need of help. We might equally feel "very well"—comfortably happy, meaningful, and productive as a family and as individual members within a family. We might call that "very sick" feeling a -3 on a continuum; feeling "very well" would be a +3. Between the two we have the possibility of feeling "sick" (-2), "a little sick" (-1), genuinely "on the fence" (0), "a little well" (+1), or "well" (+2). In all honesty, most of us feel "fine" most of the time (not a bad answer to that inquiry of the day after all!)—in the range of -1 to +1, "a little sick" to "a little well."

The continuum might look like this:

-3	-2	-1	0	+1	+2	+3
sick zone			moderate zone			well zone

We rather easily float from one zone to another, depending on the day, our health, and other circumstances. We might be in one zone for less than an hour. On the other hand, we might stay in one general zone for a year or more.

All of us have a yearning for wellness that is as natural as the healing of a wound. That yearning pulls us in a positive direction. We also have a vulnerability toward sickness that sometimes seems hard to fight. The purpose of family ministry then is to nurture us toward greater wellness and fullness in Christ so that we may better serve each other.

Like any organism, the family feels most well when it is in a state of balance—balance between its parts, balance within its functions, and balance with its outside environment. A family bombarded by outside stress is thrown off balance. Sudden unemployment, loss of a home by fire or storm, neighborhood break-ins, or increased demands of job, community, or school upset the balance of a family. Off-balance, we feel "not so well." Like a small-town driver in the middle of Chicago traffic, we seek refuge—a place where we can safely stop, relax, read a road map over a cup of coffee, and get our bearings. Upset by environmental stress over which we may have little or no control, we need support and direction.

We can be thrown off balance from within a family structure as well. The death of a spouse, for example, shakes up and shocks a family—throws it way off balance. The loss of a family member will often draw a whole extended family unit together to support and heal the wounds of real "sickness." During the aftermath of the shock, during the anger, grief, and acceptance of loss, a family struggles to gain balance in its new form. Coming from a family of nine siblings, I remember "sick" feelings of sadness and anxiety within the family even at the natural loss of each child who reached 18. Additions can do the same. The system has to accommodate each new member. Mixed with all the excitement over a new baby is also the stress of extra tasks, new demands, and jealous siblings. A major change from within, whether it be a loss or a gain, will temporarily throw a family system off-balance and even move it into a zone of "sickness."

Any one member experiencing change or distress will also shake the family system. Both of my children went through strange regressions and downright orneriness the August before their first years of school. I may already have been dealing with my own anxieties about letting go; this added disorder threw me completely off-balance. I was never so relieved to see them off to school so I could get on with a new pattern and sense of equilibrium. A perspective of humor and the experience of a friend did much to get me through those weeks. (She had come home one day to discover one of her almost-first-graders sucking a bottle!) Her ministry in simple terms pointed me in the direction of healing. And this was merely a simple developmental shift in the family!

A teething baby, a bed-wetting child, an eight-year-old socialite, a member suffering illness or injury, a 16-year-old driver, an adolescent searching for identity, a parent in mid-life crisis—any one of these can put internal stress on a family and upset its balance and feelings of wellness.

To feel well a family needs some sense of balance—balance within and between its members and balance with its environment. In more positive terms, a family needs some sense of closeness, some shared meaning, some common interests and decisions, and a general feeling of support and unity. This comes from a balance between the needs of the family as a unit and the needs of individuals within the family. Each family member needs to feel special and unique, but each also needs to be part of a family that they can feel good about. And each member needs to feel good in him/herself.

Within my family I feel good when some decisions are mine to make and others are agreed on as a family. I feel good when I know I am supported and yet am responsible for my own actions. I feel good knowing that I belong, yet knowing that I am also on my own, contributing and sharing outside the family in ways that are uniquely me. I don't feel good when I am restricted, locked into a rigid role, belonging only to the family with nothing left for me. I don't feel good when I am not supported, not "connected" in some way to another.

The balance of the two—individuality and unity—is a zone of wellness. This sense of closeness and togetherness—how a family *is* together, the spirit of the family—is the wellness of the body of Christ, joined in Christ to build each other up and to praise God with individual talents. It is this body that needs to be in balance to feel well together in Christ.

There is perhaps no clearer image of this healthy togetherness than in Paul's description of the church as body:

> For just as the body is one and has many members, and all the members of the body, though many, are one body, so it is with Christ. For by one Spirit we are all baptized into one body—Jews or Greeks, slaves or free—and all were made to drink of one Spirit.
>
> For the body does not consist of one member but of many. If the foot should say, "Because I am not a hand, I do not belong to the body," that would not make it any less a part of the body. And if the ear should say, "Because I am not an eye, I do not belong to the body," that would not make it any less a part of the body. If the whole body were an eye, where would be the hearing? If the whole body were an ear, where would be the sense of smell? But as it is, God arranged the organs in the body, each one of them, as he chose. (1 Cor. 12:12-18)

So it is with family. Few siblings are exactly or even nearly the same. What makes us one is not our sameness but the spirit of togetherness that binds us in love and respect to each other as individuals.

During a low point in my marriage, I wondered how I could ever have married someone so different from myself and how I could be so much the opposite of my daughter. That I felt a need to be the same in order to be united with my husband and my children was itself a symptom of not being quite "well." I didn't feel well in the family unit until I could appreciate each of us in our differentness and yet celebrate our unity, seeing our separate purposes. I can delight and find security in my husband's gregarious nature. I can admire my daughter's blunt and sometimes impulsive honesty that has more than once been of aid to the family. And they can enjoy and appreciate my separate contributions to the family. We are united not because we are the same but because we are joined in love to each other. Balance within means a balance of unity and individuality, of closeness and separateness.

Families can be thrown off balance by how they function too. How a family gets things done is a basic dimension of family systems. Members of a family may feel "sick" when everything is confusing and chaotic, or when authoritarian order is rigidly imposed. It is especially disorienting and dis-easing when families pretend that everything is OK on the surface, yet everyone feels not so well on the inside; there is orderliness and structure on the surface but chaos within. A structured yet flexible family feels good to most.

Notice how extremely rigid or extremely chaotic structures affect the function of family discipline, for example. Children who grow up without the rules and values of a family often feel confused; the only way to gain approval is to "please." Children growing up in families run by strict order without room for negotiating or testing limits are often equally bothered; they are set up to fail because they can never live up to the rigid demands. Ironically, children from both extremes often end up with the same low self-esteem and shame—"not well" feelings. Those who grow up in confusion feel shame for wrongs they are not sure of, those from rigid homes for the numerous inevitable infringements. The confused can hardly internalize standards and values they never experienced; the others try to get away with whatever is possible when authority isn't looking. Obviously, the issue of wellness for families isn't whether permissiveness or law and order is correct. "Wellness" is a balance between the two that feels most comfortable and accomplishes the needed tasks within each particular unique family.

When leadership is dependable yet democratic enough to allow everyone some control and responsibility, each family member feels capable—at age 2, 12, 35, and 80. This feels good. When discipline is consistent, fair, and connected with natural consequences, children and adults learn healthy guilt and responsibility for their actions: "I'm sorry that I hurt you" and "I will pick up the pieces." When issues can be renegotiated with new situations and new information, each family member feels respected and capable of solving problems. This too feels good.

Families that can tend to daily tasks and daily order with a spirit of cooperation, respect for leadership, and dedication to some common and solid values feel "well." If we merge the two dimensions—how families are together and how families get things done—we come up with some sense of what wellness might mean: a family in which the members are close but not all the same and that goes about daily tasks and family maintenance with structured yet flexible freedom.

You will find no greater model of this wellness than in the Biblical images of Christ and His disciples: Jesus the Master washes the feet of His disciples; Christ the Head values each member of the body; each is called by name and given unique talents, yet each is united in a singular task and story. Such a model helps us see that balance comes not from an outside vision of an "ideal" family but from the inner source of God's purpose—His Spirit, being "in Christ," having "God with us." It grows and maintains balance from acts of care, acceptance, love, and forgiveness—from life lived in grace. The Law and the Gospel offer the fullest image of the structured yet flexible freedom of wellness.

Each family will search out its own particular place in these dimensions of togetherness and task, a place that feels best—most well—to them. For a family with rich traditions of structure, that place may be more ordered and close-knit than for another. For a family that has known independence yet strong respect for others, that comfortable place may be more separate and flexible. For the single-parent family, that place might be less formally structured yet emotionally closer in the parent-child relationship.

And the place will shift as the family changes, as new situations arise, and as individual members change. Families with young children, for example, often feel best when family life is more structured than flexible and when close support is either immediately or consistently available. As our children grew older, however, we naturally moved toward more individual autonomy and a more flexible structure; that seemed quite naturally more "well" to us.

This constantly shifting dynamic of a search for balance is sometimes uncomfortable or even difficult for a family. It can be hard to shift set patterns that worked well at one time even if they no longer feel comfortable. One member of the family may particularly want or need to stay with a pattern that no longer seems best for the other individuals in the family or for the family as a whole. Searching for a healthy new balance may require the supportive ministry of others with insight and care. The drive for wellness is there, but it may be blocked by other complicating factors or by mere habit.

Even when a family knows and chooses its own place in the "wellness zone," forces from within and without can jar the system. We may have a clear perception of health and wellness for our family. We may even have open communication, clear understanding of the boundaries of each member's role, and healthy give and take—all characteristics of healthy, functioning families. Yet persistent strains, transitions, changes, and rather ordinary weaknesses or deficits in our lives can disturb family balance. Quite simply, this is stress.Stress makes families vulnerable to sickness just as surely as negative patterns in the dimensions of family systems.

Because we are so often pulled out of balance by excessive stress, much of ministry to families involves providing ongoing resources to handle it. Studies in stress management have taught us that basic to our ability to cope with stress is our belief system. Even if there has been no recognized involvement in ministry to families in stress, surely this ministry is central to the church.

Emotional mastery—often defined as feeling "at one with oneself" (and I would add "at one with God")—is equally basic. Emotional mastery comes as an outgrowth of meditation or prayer. Again, in this form of ministry the church can be and perhaps has been a powerful resource to each family member. I grew up with both of these resources. They gave me a strong base for coping with stress.

But they weren't always enough in the distress of crisis. They weren't always enough in situations of persistent pressure. Receiving support from others and understanding ourselves and our situation are equally important in handling stress. Support systems give us perspective by sharing common experience. They strengthen us with the encouragement that comes both from within us and from others who relate to us. Understanding reduces our anxieties by helping us see more clearly. When we better understand ourselves and our situation, we are better able to cope. Both of these resources are equally essential to ministry to families in stress. Ongoing ministry tc families within our congregations and to the family that is our congregation needs to include resources that reduce, not add to, stress. Do we put greater stress on our family members and their households, or do we provide important resources to handle stress?

Because of stress, natural changes, crises, and the dynamic dimensions of family systems, most of us move along the continuum of wellness, sometimes quite well yet inevitably sometimes quite sick too. Ministry to families therefore needs to be comprehensively aimed at nurturing families toward greater wellness.

How can this be done? Because of the many aspects of family wellness, ministry within family needs to happen in three modes: support, education, and enrichment.

In times of greatest crisis and greatest sickness, a family needs support. Support involves empathy, concrete help, and nurturing toward independence. After a fire, a family needs immediate relief: clothing, lodging, and emergency support. Empathetic listening to the grief and anger and help with the difficult decision making that comes in the aftermath of such a loss is next in line and just as important. With ongoing help to rebuild or relocate and to refurnish a new home, a family is finally nurtured toward independence again. This model of support ministry is equally valid for crises of relationship or personal trauma. Alcoholics Anonymous and Al-Anon are built on this recognition. Shelters for battered women and rape crisis centers operate with a similar awareness. In extreme crisis we need empathetic support. The goal is always, however, to move on to greater wellness and less dependence on others. Hopefully, one can then in turn give support to others in similar crises. Support ministry is crucial to families and individuals in the -2 and -3 "sickness zone."

Education ministry is most needed in the mid-range zones where our feeling is "I guess things are OK." Learning more about preschool children and parenting was very helpful for me when I worried about behaviors between two toddlers and in many ways neglected my husband in excessive concern about infant development. Even more helpful was information about overactive allergic children that was shared with me in a noncritical way when I struggled with the exhausting behaviors of my oldest. In the context of empathetic support from a Christian woman who had lived for 21 years with a hyperactive son, this education ministry gave me a new vision of parenting that led to greater wellness in our family system.

By providing images of healthy patterns, education ministry can move us again in the direction of wellness. By anticipating patterns and experiences, education at key transitions or turning points in our life can also enhance wellness. There is now enough evidence in the study of human behavior to confirm that prenatal classes, premarital instruction, divorce-adjustment groups, and preretirement courses help people handle each transition with greater comfort and satisfaction—with greater wellness.

The enrichment mode of ministry is often the least recognized because it is the hardest to define and tends to serve those who are already living in zones of some wellness. We wonder if it is not simply icing on the cake that we ought to do without. It is indeed not a helpful focus for those in critical need or crisis. When one is starving, a recipe for whole wheat bread or vegetable meat loaf, or even the offer of the use of a kitchen range will hardly suffice! Intentional enrichment of families begins at a point of less critical need when one has the wheat, the meat, and the oven—at -1 on the continuum—and it *continues* toward the wellness end of the scale. Enrichment ministry assumes that within each family, within each person, there is untapped potential that can grow in an environment of relating and working openly with others, in an environment of enjoying, sharing, practicing new skills, and imagining new possibilities.

In secular terms, vacation is enrichment; it renews and refreshes by simply giving us the opportunity to be in a different environment, experience, or schedule. A retreat is enrichment; it renews our spirit. It adds nothing to what isn't already planted within us, yet it leads to far greater wellness. A structured opportunity for couples to share feelings, thoughts, and needs with each other is enrichment; it adds nothing that isn't already potentially within the relationship, yet it leads to greater intimacy and wellness. Enrichment ministry strengthens families from their unique point of wellness—from "where they are at"—and truly builds up the body of Christ as it nurtures growth.

All three modes—support, education, and enrichment—are needed to fully and comprehensively minister to families. The uniqueness of Christian ministry is not in these three modes or even in a notion of wellness, however. Because the family is the body of Christ, Christian ministry is *mutual* ministry, that we may be filled "with all the fullness of God" (Eph. 3:19).

The direction toward wellness in life "in Christ" is far greater than psychological, emotional, or physical wellness. Nurturing families in the faith, building up the body of Christ, is growth toward *fullness in Christ.* We are called to new life in Christ (Eph. 4—6). We are to put on "the new nature, created after the likeness of God in true righteousness and holiness" (Eph. 4:24).

This call is consistent with the natural leaning toward wellness, yet it goes beyond it. It is a call in the midst of daily family relationships. The Ephesians images are specific—friends, children, parents, husbands, wives, living in daily honesty, respect, and praise of God.

This is also a call to mutual ministry. We are urged to grow as a body, to join together "in love" (Eph. 4:16), to help others in need (v. 28), to "be subject to one another out of reverence for Christ" (5:21), and to be friends with one another. In sum, it is a call "to equip the saints for the work of ministry, for building up the body of Christ, until we all attain to the unity of the faith and of the knowledge of the Son of God, to mature manhood, to the measure of the stature of the fullness of Christ" (4:12-13). This is an image of family wellness that has no end! Nurturing in the faith in daily familial reality is important at every point on the continuum and beyond, into service, mission, and fullness in Christ!

4. How Broad Is This Ministry?

The full breadth of family ministry touches all those in our midst in all of life at all stages—from birth through death in all life situations. Is it an impossible task?

It does seem unthinkable if not impossible to meet all needs of all people. Perhaps that is why, in almost every congregation I have been a part of, people seem to "fall between the cracks." Plenty of programs were offered, yet none fit. I remember being too young for the youth group but too old to fit into all the fun activities of the primary group, too old for the youth group but not belonging to the young couples' club, too single to fit into couple activities when my husband's work kept him from full participation in our own church yet not single enough for singles' groups. With a bit of humor, I fit best into a Dr. Seuss classic: "too fancy . . . too bumpy . . . too curly . . . too lumpy!" With a "plug-in" mode of ministry, I will never find a power source! There is never an outlet that quite fits my design.

So long as we think of family ministry simply in terms of programs filling every slot, the task is insurmountable, and many will not find a place. There will never be enough hours in the week or in the month to provide programs to fit everyone, not to mention the "burn-out" that the staff would experience. Yet family ministry is to encompass all. Surely this is impossible!

It might help, first of all, to open up possibilities other than just programs. What other forms can ministry take? In order not to neglect even one member of God's family, we surely need to open all avenues of one-to-one, one-to-some, and one-to-all ministry; we need to extend forms of church-family ministry beyond simply offering programs. Perhaps more ministry can happen in the worship setting, in the narthex, in the parking lot, and in our homes, without always scheduling programs. This reframing alone could bring our task into the range of possibility. Besides, the task is to minister to each, not to provide a program for each.

Even so, the task of ministering from birth till death seems enormous. Perhaps we can neglect or just skip over ministry to some ages. We all know that certain stages of life seem harder. We could simply focus on these. After all, in the long run we will touch everyone at least once in his/her life if we offer a Sunday school curriculum for the very young, youth programs and confirmation instruction for our teens, pastoral counseling around weddings and funerals, and maybe a Bible study—and worship, of course—for the adults (or at least for the women). But what is it like to be five and wonder if Grandpa is growing wings in heaven? How do we make sense of God as a 10-year-old skeptic? What is it like to really begin to take on adult roles as father or mother, as worker, or as an adult member of a Christian community? How does one reevaluate the whole meaning of life in connection with pregnancy—or infertility? Is there any Christian understanding or support during mid-life doubts and changes? Where are we when the always reliable woman of the church fears that she is physically faltering with age? Each of these unique points of development or crisis is a point of ministry. Somehow as a church we need to be there at that time. Church-family ministry means ministry throughout the life cycle, in every developmental stage along the way. Even our intentional design needs to include the total life-span and all common life situations and crises. So we are back to an impossible task!

Well then, we must skip some of the particular life situations! But which ones?—the hurts that are least common? the people with rare diseases? crib deaths? the family with a troubled youth or hyperactive child? those going through divorce (we still have relatively few of those in our congregations)? the sorely disillusioned or disappointed? the senile? the families providing intensive home nursing care for a parent? the single parent? the unemployed? the teenage alcoholic? the teenage parent? the child who comes to church alone? These may all be less common, but it seems embarrassing if not foolish to ignore them when we see them listed in print.

There seems to be no way around it. The church uniquely knows and cares for total families at all ages and in all life stages. Somehow we must minister to them in all these situations. The ministry *is* enormous; the task is great. Ministry to families means ministry in every crisis and stage along the way—ministry that validates each in his/her own unique person and cares for each.

As a mother, I can appreciate the enormity of this task. I also find myself occasionally burdened by the size of the job. Nurse, cook, counselor, chauffeur, shopper, etc.—there are far too many tasks for any one woman, even Super-Mom! I can't do all that! How can I ease the task? I discover that when I ask the whole family to be involved, the task is not so huge. Nurturing, care, and maintenance within the family must be shared to be manageable at all. We can make the task of ministry to families in our congregation equally manageable. Were we to share this ministry among ourselves, perhaps the task would not be so great. Involving all members of our congregations will ease the burden on a few and make much more possible.

This requires more vision than skill. When I ask my 10-year-old son to help with a family task, I want him to fold clothes, mow the lawn, or attend his sister's concert; I don't ask him to drive the car. He is able to help and care for others in his family not with a lot of motherly skill but with his 10-year-old skills. With them, he can be a part of the family. It is his notion of belonging to a family, his love, and his sense of responsibility that make him a part of our family ministry. The same is true in our congregations. In love and responsiveness each member can be an integral part of the total church ministry to the family—as each is able.

This not only makes the task manageable. It changes our very attitude toward the task. When the jobs at home are "Mom's," others merely "help Mom." This does little to ease the burden that I feel. When the job is mine, I may delegate tasks, but the responsibility and burden remain forever mine. Furthermore, Mom is doing something "for others"—waiting on others, cleaning up after others, feeding others, and constantly supporting others. Likewise, when the tasks of church belong to a few, we merely do for others or help the few. When we minister because we love, belong, and want to respond, we are really acting as responsible members of the family. In family love we will care for each other not because we were assigned someone else's task but because that is what it means to belong to a family.

Within the Christian community, ministry to the family is unique in that it hinges on our very notion of the church. In ministering to families within our congregations, we are not ministering to "others."

We belong to a family. Out of love and the responsibility of belonging, we minister to each other. We are building up and caring for our own family members, for the church itself is the family of God. Notice that the hurt of one is inevitably the hurt of all. Just as an injured child affects a whole family system, an injured family affects the whole community of God's people—the whole family of God. You must have noticed, for example, the effect that a divorce, a death, or a troubled youth can have on a whole congregation. A congregation that is ministering to families is always healing itself and ministering to its own.

Church-family ministry takes on greater significance when we recognize that together we are the body of Christ. It then becomes important to support the single parent; to lend guidance to the delinquent youth, the irritated parent, and the confused and anxious spouse or spouse-to-be; to feed the hungry and unemployed; to stand by the grieving widow; to protect the abused child and the battered wife; and to move all toward greater "wellness" and fuller service in Christ. As each person grows in wellness in Christ, we all together grow in fullness as a body with Christ as the Head.

We are covenanted to each other and to God. We are not "others." We are born into the covenant, and we die in it. From birth till death we are unique individuals in the household of God. The covenant makes us members of a family, the body of Christ. We must not be forgotten at any age, in any crisis, or in any strange corner. In individual congregations we are called to live out that covenant. Surely God does not neglect even one of His own; neither can we afford to neglect even one. So broad is our ministry.

This covenant vision changes our whole attitude toward family ministry. We are bonded by God's covenant act of history and promise. By God's act we are made brothers and sisters in Christ. Primary family ties can help us understand this better. As siblings by family covenant, our children may squabble and compete in the home, but somehow each will come to the other's aid when a teacher seems unfair or a bully picks a fight. Long after we leave our childhood homes, we feel bonded to our siblings in spite of distance or even differing degrees of compatibility. We will both grieve and celebrate with them for a total lifetime. Family creates a bond, a covenant. It is much the same for covenant people of God. We are bonded. The happiness and pain of each member is ours as well. This is so whether we actually take part in it or not. I have missed family reunions; that makes me no less a member of my family. I have missed Sunday worship; neither does that make me less a member of the covenant people of God. To see ourselves as covenanted to God and to each other is to see ourselves as family—never as "others" to whom we must minister.

So the task is mutual care of each other as each is called or able—a shared ministry out of love, a sense of belonging, and covenant responsibility. To share this vision is to include all in family ministry—and to do so in the context of all.

Ministry to one, to some, and to all is always integrated into the total family. We are ultimately family, joined together in spite of different talents, age, or need. Even when we focus separately on households, peer groups, or those with other common needs, we cannot remove them from the congregational family unit. Within any institution it is easy to segment tasks. (Larger institutions may be particularly vulnerable to this.) Thus confirmation ministry is a separate task of the pastor, not really the concern of others or of any other separate area such as youth education. Families in need of crisis support may be in our communion, but they are really the focus of the counseling pastor, as are premarrieds and those involved in private Christian instruction. There is a committee that takes care of visiting or mailing greetings to our hospitalized or shut-ins; a group gathers somewhere in the church for support as singles; and so on. Somehow each ministry is easily slotted into a separate cubbyhole and never receives total community concern or response. When issues or concerns arise, we can be tempted to pull people aside and minister to their needs off in some quiet corner of congregational life. Yet all of this *is* a part of the mainstream. In meeting specialized needs we need also to lend support and ministry within the total community of which they are members. In developing specialized programs, we need to keep them always a part of the total worship, education, and fellowship life. In focusing on particular concerns and in ministering to particular individuals, we need to keep them in context of community.

I'm not talking about public exposure of each one's hurts or needs, public confession, or having only total community gatherings. I am talking about community prayers, community celebration, community service, and shared community ministry. I'm talking about congregational awareness and involvement in all aspects of education, support, and enrichment. I'm talking about open support for each other as families and as individuals. I'm talking about living in fellowship, knowing and caring for each other as family. The most effective ministry to families happens in the supportive context of the community as each is openly acknowledged, supported, and nurtured as individuals and households in the family of God.

In this regard, ministry to the family is as broad and as deep as the congregational community itself. Everything within its midst and everything within each unit falls into its range. In mutual ministry to each other, this is what Christian fellowship can be.

Yet ministry to the family goes beyond this. Built up in service to Christ, we are called to reach beyond our own community. Within the Kingdom of God we are to feed the hungry, clothe the naked, and visit the sick and imprisoned (Matt. 25:31-46). By Christ's command we are to go to "all nations" (Matt. 28:18-20). We are to "show hospitality to strangers, . . . remember those who are in prison, . . . and those who are ill-treated, since you also are in the body" (Heb. 13:2-3). Ultimately, "love your neighbor" goes beyond the walls of each local church. So does our ministry to the family. There is reason to consider how we as congregations can minister to the family in our community, nation, and world.

In practical terms, this is also a ministry toward wellness—wellness in body, mind, and spirit as we work toward health, equality, and freedom in our community and in the world. This is often a ministry to the poor, the oppressed, and those in crisis. It is often a ministry against injustice and repression. In the broader context of community we have a call to live as Christ—healing, feeding, teaching, proclaiming His love and forgiveness in word and deed, and calling others into service. The breadth of this ministry has no end and will be selected and shaped by each congregation.

This ministry is as broad as the handiwork of God's creation, for creation itself is part of our family. Living in a family relationship with all of creation is part of our responsibility as people of God. This final sensitivity in ministry to family is a part of all of our forms of family ministry. It affects our baptizing one of God's creatures; it is a part of our building committee's decision in response to needs for different education or parking facilities; it is a part of our worship atmosphere; and it is a part of the nurturing education and the service ministry of both youth and adults. Ministry to the family means ministering to all of God's creation.

Ministry to the family is broad, but the purpose is not to establish a perfect or even a totally complete ministry. The purpose of ministry to families is to nurture them toward greater wellness and fullness in Christ. When a total community of faith—a congregation together with the church at large—is dedicated to each member and sensitive to all people and all creation, such a comprehensive ministry is imaginable, even possible.

In practical reality, how broad is family ministry likely to be within any one congregation? We are obviously limited by time and energy, by staff, and by finances and facilities. This is precisely why sharing some vision of the breadth of full family ministry is so important. Unless we as a total community of faith have a vision of the potentially wide range of ministry to the family, we are likely to narrow our sights to a few interested families or to a few we mark as being in need. In response to the obvious crisis needs in our communities, we may feel embarrassed or guilty about ministering to ourselves instead of to the hurt or hungry around us. Usually we can more easily muster support for a need "out there" than we can for the same needs within our own congregation. Recognizing ourselves as the body of Christ helps us recognize also the need to nurture and support each member of the body so that we can indeed be a stronger body of Christ active in the world. It is not selfish to feed our children nutritional food; in fact, it better equips them to be of vigorous service in the world. Hopefully, we can minister both to the immediate members of our family and to our more distant brothers and sisters.

Ministry to the family should support each member of our congregation as he/she relates in a primary caring and nurturing family unit. It should open doors of ministry to all families within the congregation. It should also reach out to families in our immediate local community in areas in which we are most capable. And this ministry should keep us all sensitive to our relationship to all of God's children and creation.

The possibilities are far-reaching. Some of all these levels of ministry will happen in congregations that see a need for ministry to people and their relationships within the family of God.

5. How Do We Go About Developing a More Intentional Church-Family Ministry?

There is clearly a need for intentional ministry to the family within our congregations. We are also clearly on solid theological and traditional ground in venturing into such ministry. What remains to be seen is just how we can enact this ministry within the wide variety of Christian congregations throughout the country.

The Christian church is a church of Word, community, and service. This is the very foundation and premise most needed for ministry to the family. It implies that the seeds for church-family ministry already lie within each congregation. The task is not to "sell a new package." It is rather to awaken a ministry that is already inherent in the Christian community.

For most congregations, no radical restructuring will be needed. In implementing a ministry to the family, most will discover much that is already happening in that area. The emphasis will be to become more aware, more intentional, and more holistic in what has long been important to congregations. To respond most completely to families, congregations may desire to join with others in a cluster and thus broaden their resources. They may also connect with broader resources of the church in an ongoing partnership. They will probably discover new strengths and dimensions of lay ministry within their own community, and in the act of ministry to the family, most will discover far-reaching avenues of service.

The process of developing church-family ministry is simple and exciting in itself. Nine steps are proposed here, which can be dealt with in a group of concerned laity, in a study of service by the congregation as a whole, or in the context of a cooperative cluster of congregations. The time needed will vary with each parish, and the final design will certainly be unique to each.

Step 1: *Brainstorm "Ministry to Family."* We each carry an agenda and certain notions in our heads. Many a good program or process has been buried or thwarted by unattended agenda. It is most helpful to begin any new process with an open brainstorm. We need to know what is out there already—the hurts, the histories, the needs, the premises, the assumptions, and the private visions that can help shape or hinder our ministry.

Open brainstorm means collecting all ideas about ministry to the family—what that means most immediately to people. It is possible to use a survey to collect this information, but it is preferable to join together in time and space to brainstorm spontaneously. Often our most immediate response is most powerful and accurate. Given time to think, we may filter our own ideas or even develop completely predetermined visions of ministry. This can only hinder a full, open process that in the long run is most responsive and creative.

You will need large sheets of paper, a fast hand, and receptivity to every idea thrown at you. This is not a time for filtering or judgment. It is a time for open sharing where all are heard and everything is recorded. Common issues, ideas, and concerns will emerge. Circle these for future reference and save everything.

Step 2: *Study Scripture.* Any ministry needs a Scriptural and theological base. Parishioners will respond best to a ministry when they discover this for themselves. Few of us really like to be told what to do, what to believe, or what to think. Look at the Scriptural and theological foundation of the family together. Who is family in Scripture? What does it mean to be family? What is our theological vision of family?

Studies of family are available. Chapter One of this handbook might be a good place to start. Explore texts on the family in open dialog.

Here are some groups of passages that might be especially considered:

1. Ps. 8; 24:1-2; 95:1-7; 148; Romans 8:19-22; Eph. 3:15—Here we see the broadest definition of family as all of God's creation. By what means?
2. Ps. 122:8-9; Is. 25:6-7—What people are God's family?
3. 1 Kings 8:14-21; Ps. 29:11; 68:9-10; 94:14-15; Is. 43:6-7—How would we define God's family according to this group of passages? Does this invalidate the former definition?
4. Matt. 12:46-50; Romans 8:14-17; 1 Tim. 5:1-2; 1 John 3:1-2—Who are the family of God, the fellow heirs with Christ, in the New Testament?
5. Ezra 2:3, 64; Ps. 96:7-8; John 19:25-27; Eph. 5:21—6:4—What is the smallest unit of family in Scripture? What makes them family?

Explore all of the questions and ideas that emerge from these texts. Search out other passages, and reflect on the message presented in Scripture as a whole. These texts will give people some sense of the multiple definitions and of the active and inclusive nature of family in Scripture.

For more focus, the book of Ephesians is an excellent source for a Bible study on the family. In it we see the inclusive definition of family, the Scriptural function and purpose of the family, the importance of the body of Christ, and the mission and challenge for all of us (e.g., "Awake, O sleeper" [5:14]—be aware).

In small groups let parishioners study the passages and recall Bible history—types of families and the purpose of the family throughout the Scriptures. Then, most importantly, share the understanding of family in their own Christian experience. Ideas can be taught, but we learn more when we discover and share. Give people time to explore and discover in open dialog, and a theological vision of family will emerge.

In study and dialog folks discover and recall what it means to be the covenant people of God. Sociological functions of the family change, in Scripture as well as in contemporary history.

It is exciting to discover that the purpose of the family—to be the people of God—remains constant. That discovery in itself can give meaning and support to families as they shape new ways of relating as God's people in times of rapid changes in role and task.

Steps 1 and 2 can be initiated and implemented by clergy and/or a few interested lay leaders prior to any decision to develop a church-family ministry. (The regular Sunday morning adult class, for example, is a likely structure for Bible study, though it may have little impact if only a few participate, and if leaders are not involved.) Together, these steps raise an awareness of the family and its place within and as the church. The interest and the numbers should increase significantly by the third step, which is obviously more accurate when there is broader input.

Step 3: *Define family within your own congregation.* It is an important early step to designate and define family specifically within each congregation, including everyone. This is important in itself—to discover family as households, as congregation, as humankind, and as all creation and to identify our personal relationship to each. But the process also reveals "hidden families," unnoticed because they are out of the mainstream of traditional activities or definitions.

How each congregation denotes family may vary. Recognizing family as all God's creation was something quite different to me in an urban surrounding, for example, than it was when I grew up on a Wisconsin farm. Likewise, family as community of faith looks quite different in each congregation: the family of a church of 2,000 contrasts significantly with that in a church of 200. Even family as household units of nurture and care is different in each congregation. Many of our rural congregations list high percentages of elderly as households; suburban churches lean just as heavily toward young two-parent families; and our urban churches are filled with high percentages of single adult households.

In this step congregations need to discover who they are as family and what are their unique households.

Step 4: *Understand family.* To be effective in our ministry to the family, more than the counseling clergy need to be aware of the family as a system. How family operates has implications for what happens in Sunday school, worship, youth groups, and in everything else that we do together as families.

An academic study of a topic as abstract as the family system will frighten even the college educated in your parish. It can be tempting to skip this step, but that would be a mistake.

We all live in a family system. We may not know big words or be able to label abstract ideas, but we surely know the family system. And we know what it feels like to be "well" or "not so well." This experience can help members learn more about the family as a system.

Try connecting people together with strings. Group five people together as a "family." Hand them a set of 20 strings, all of varying lengths, and ask them to connect themselves as a family. The first thing they will learn (not at all surprising to those who live in larger families) is that all the strings will be used. Ask what else they notice, and someone will point out that they are connected at different distances. Let them share how that feels and discover what that "system" can do or look like. Now suggest that a family member get sick—drop down, lean on others, demonstrate weakness. What happens? Strings are pulled; every string feels stress; the group may have to restructure. Try having a family member not cooperating, rebelling, or pulling heavily on one other member. Try having a family member leaving home or bringing in a new close friend or even new family members. This group should now understand what it means that the family is a system.

The dynamics of how we get things done and how we function together can also be learned from our own experience. Something that can help people understand the family is the mobile (an object that is much like an organism or a system). Families may enjoy making mobiles that look like their unique family system. In the very process of working together they discover for themselves the dimensions of *adaptability* (how we get things done) and *cohesion* (how we function together). The finished mobiles not only reveal the unique image of each family; they validate each family member as an individual figure and demonstrate how a family does or does not balance (a discovery of "wellness" dynamics). As families share mobiles, they further discover how their family system feels to them and more clearly understand "wellness" as described in Chapter 3.

Learning abstract ideas can happen even in multigenerational groups. Kindergarten twins were two of the most perceptive learners in a family "Understanding Us" course for which my husband and I served as resource persons a few years ago. We "know" the experience of family; understanding it is mostly a matter of making sense of that experience.

You might want to use social resources within or even outside your congregation in Step 4. You might need to use helpful written resources (the numerous excellent books on family). In so doing it is important to see that learning happens when it is connected with experience and when it involves more than a few selected adults.

You may discover that when you explore a ministry, you are already well into it. Step 4 in itself may help some families, and even the congregation as a whole, grow in "wellness." As we better understand a system, we can better balance and nurture it. Let Step 4 be a fun learning project in itself. Dare to involve people of all ages, total family units, and particularly youth. This is often a step of empathetic support, humor, and shared experience.

Step 5: *Determine the scope of ministry to family needed in your congregation.* The inherent premise of the scope in most congregations is that ministry is from birth to death. What does that mean for your congregation? More specifically, what does it mean for family ministry?

First of all, what is the nature of the total life cycle? Birth, obviously, is a good beginning. That usually connects with baptismal ministry. What about a ministry of helping the family adjust to the infant? Preschool age might come next. The developmental childhood years are usually easy to identify. Chances are your Sunday school program already has these well segregated and labeled. Youth—there's a big one! Every year seems to deserve special consideration. What are the significant stages in the life cycle from age 12 to 21? Adulthood is where the life cycle seemingly ends in many parishes. Once people are married, the next stage is buried! Yet adulthood is broadly rich in life stages. Popular labels like "mid-life crisis" have helped alert us to the incredible range of the adult life cycle. A growing number of assertive elderly are likewise awakening us to the importance of life after retirement. What are all the imaginable life cycle stages in your congregational family experience?

You might do well to list those stages in a long column on the left side of a large sheet of paper. Include all possibilities at first. Later you can combine or omit as you compare the list with the profile of your own congregation. You will discover that some life events are significantly common to different ages (e.g., divorce, death of a child or a spouse, unemployment). List these also. You might discover other themes that thread through a number of stages, such as sexual development, grief, or facing death. Include these too—either as ongoing threads or where you notice that they particularly emerge. Your final list should highlight those life events that are most common in your congregation, but don't omit any significant stages in the life cycle.

Ministry itself has three modes or forms: support, education, and enrichment (see Chapter 3). Write these across the top of your sheet, and you have a handy chart illustrating the full range and scope of ministry to the family as you see it in your congregation. The following sample chart shows how this listing might appear. Additional categories may be added.

Life Stages	Support	Education	Enrichment
Birth			
—infancy			
Preschool			
Elementary age			
Teen			
—identity			
Young adult			
—life-style			
Marriage			
—courtship			
—sexuality			
—marriage adjustment			
—beginning family			
—ongoing life together			
Divorce			
Singles			
—single parent			
Mid-life			
—in marriage			
—in career			
—in family changes			
Preretirement			
Retirement years			
Grandparenthood			
[etc.]			

Step 6: *Identify the needs.* "I know what you need" won't work here.

As a parent I often presume to know what is best for my children, and I will solidly defend that I am probably quite right. I need to be disarmed by their expressions of their own needs. Their "I need a hug" disarms *my* need to lecture. "All I need is a piece of paper" disarms *my* need to oversee their school work. I assume that my volatile 12-year-old will need help in making her wishes and hurts tactfully known in a strained friendship; she disarms me with her tactfully assertive phone conversation with her friend.

In my supportive parenting, I am *sure* that my son needs help in searching out and designing his project for the area science fair—but he needs neither! Then in my certainty of his need for support, I bolster him up in anticipation of disappointment over the judging—but he doesn't need that either. The pride of his self-earned blue ribbon is his, and I suspect he would have handled the disappointment of no accolade on his own too.

We dare not presume to know another's needs. Studying issues and learning more about life stages and crises is important and necessary. We need to know the expressed and perceived needs of the elderly, the widowed, the divorced, the adolescent, the incest victim, the bereaved. We need to use all the resources at our disposal; we need a better understanding of these needs. But ultimately, we also need to hear each member, each life-stage group, and each person in a unique crisis share their felt needs.

Identify the needs that you hear shared, perceived, and expressed—needs correlating with each life stage that is listed in your left-hand column. Search out needs, ask for input from those who have had the experience, and provide comfortable, open opportunities for all to get in touch with and express their own needs. You will discover that these needs will be physical, emotional, and spiritual—the holistic uniqueness of openly sharing needs in the context of Christian community.

These needs will change. New needs will emerge and old ones will take on a different form. This must be an ongoing process that becomes a part of church-family ministry set in motion. Because of the fluctuating nature of needs, it might be best to record them on separate sheets of paper, correlating with but not a part of the chart you developed in Step 5.

Step 7: *Assess your present ministry to the family.* Use the chart you designed in Step 5. Investigate the workings of your congregation. What is already happening? Where would it fit on your chart? This is both validating and challenging as congregations discover the ministry that is already at work and recognize what yet needs to be done. Much of what is happening is good. Some of it will seem less important in the light of other major areas of concern and need you have now unearthed. And some of it may need to change—and may even begin to change as you examine the situation.

Fill in your chart with everything that seems to be a part of your support, education, or enrichment ministry to the family. Include worship, Sunday school, all Sunday education, midweek ministries, interest groups, annual events—everything that seems relevant—and don't be afraid to write something twice. You will discover multiple connections—e.g., worship is often a support, an enrichment, and even an education ministry for nearly all ages.

What more would you wish for? Continue filling in the chart with what seems possible and what is essential. (Indicate differences in priority by using parentheses or a different color of ink.) Issues, concerns, and ideas that emerged in your brainstorm in Step 1 might help you here. This is the beginning of a vision. Pull out all imaginable ideas from your congregation. Worry later about how workable or even desirable they might be. This is a time to dream.

Now begins the challenge. What ought we to be doing? Look at your chart. Are there obvious gaps? Are there areas of overdose? Should we even out our energies and efforts? join with other churches for resources? Is everything too segmented? How can we develop a holistic family ministry with no connections between ages? Note intergenerational links. How are we together? How can one group support another? How do we all connect as the one body of Christ?

This is a time for realistic assessment, for asking, What do we value most as Christians? It is a time for making new connections and developing new visions of ministry:

What are we doing?

What could we be doing?
What are we all about?

Coming out of a sensitivity toward and greater understanding of family—both as system and as people of God—Step 7 is perhaps the pivotal point of this process. To recognize the ministry is to begin acting on it. A realistic assessment together with visions of possibilities determines the form of the ministry. What follows serves this vision.

Step 8: *Explore resources.* The resources for a full church-family ministry are available—within your congregation, the church, and the community.

Your most powerful resource is the life experience of each member in your midst. Member ministering to member is at the heart of the Christian community. What do you know about each family member that could somehow fit in this ministry? Obviously, some have professional expertise or personal skills that one can enlist. All have life experiences that fit into your total picture of this holistic ministry. You don't need to do this with formal lists and assignments (though you might choose to in some cases). If the structure connects people meaningfully, people-to-people resources will be shared naturally. What is important is that *each* knows he/she is needed and called to this service and that each discovers his/her own inner and community resources.

What resource people could you further enlist from your community? from the church at large? Some congregations discover continued educational resources through church social service agencies, for example, or through networking with other area churches. Departments of parish services and ministry and Christian publishing houses are useful ongoing resources. Training programs in lay ministry might strengthen your individual members.

What are your education resources? your enrichment resources? your clergy resources? What support ministries are already available in your community—physical, social, and spiritual resources? Don't stop with the obvious. Be thorough and creative. This is a time for exploration.

Step 9: *Develop a structure and design for church-family ministry.* We end where many mistakenly begin. What seems most possible and necessary may be clear by now.

This must be a design that will work for your congregation or cluster—one that speaks to your perceived needs and one that fits the picture of who you now see yourselves to be.

I have seen congregations totally restructure to more fully minister to each other as family. I have seen congregations reframe, expand, and enrich existing structures with a vision of more intentional ministry to each other in family and households. Few congregations, once they are aware of a fuller vision of ministry to the family, are unable to come up with a design. Even where no formal structure is altered, a new intention evolves.

What might work for you? What might be possible? What media and structure do you need to convey this new vision of ministry? How could the design begin? How can the intention be set in motion?

To develop a church-family ministry is to begin a process. These nine steps, each worked out according to the character of your own congregation, can mark the beginning, not the completion, of a holistic intentional ministry to the family. The steps are a generic process, not a detailed or carefully prescribed program. Each congregation must "own" and develop its own process and final program. All of these steps, taken in order, are necessary, however. The temptation to skip steps to speed up the process will only result in a less than holistic ministry. Step by step the laity will more fully and more broadly explore, discover, and tune into resources, build each other up, and participate in what is their own envisioned ministry in Christ. It is likely that the structure that evolves will be unique to your congregation—a demonstration and enactment of your shared vision of the body of Christ in your midst, a total family ministry.

6. What Form Might This Take?

I hesitate to describe specific structures that convey intentional ministry to the family. Most of us would rather buy into a finished product or model than go through the sometimes long and difficult process of designing our own. I have more than once chosen to use a packaged course rather than bothering to develop my own. I often buy ready-made clothes. I even find packaged vacations inviting. Invariably, however, if I really want a satisfying fit, I will redesign that course, alter that garment, and lose interest in the vacation that would never quite fit my real interests or my budget. I hope that similar alterations for a better fit would be made to any model structure found worth implementing in this listing.

To encourage this kind of creative implementation, I will describe generalized forms of structure rather than specific churches or models. With this method, you will likely recognize specific congregations within your own district or community. These can then become sources for further information and research.

The purpose of exploring structure is not to discover or devise a perfect, flawless, or ideal form. If that were the case, the exploration would not be worth our effort, for—like every other invented or evolved human structure—whatever we would devise would be less than perfect, would certainly have its flaws, and would be far from ideal. Our purpose is rather to imagine and implement structures that encourage and nourish "fullness" and "wellness" in a community united as family, as the body of Christ with Christ as its Head. What structure will best facilitate and nurture the family and each member of that family in your community of faith?

With this in mind, explore these models of church structure, recognizing that most lie within an even broader church constitution and form.

Communities of Care, Faith, and Fellowship

In models not unlike the early Christian church, specifically designed *communities of care, faith, and fellowship* are structured to bring all life experience and liturgy together in total intergenerational communities of faith. Most are limited in size and require long-term commitment and dedication to the community. Lay leaders are usually trained to be sensitive to the concepts of life together in a faith community. That life together seldom means sharing living quarters; it rather implies a supportive sharing of life experiences—from eating of meals to sharing life struggles—in the face of God. Thus life and liturgy intermingle both naturally and intentionally. Life lived daily in Christ is recognized and celebrated as liturgy. Traditional church functions such as worship, education, and mission become part of the natural flow of family life—much as storytelling, learning, prayer, singing, and family tasks are a part of many family households. Most of what happens occurs naturally in an intergenerational community.

Because of their limited size and the high degree of commitment, specially established communities of care and fellowship usually know and respond well to each member. Most are very interpersonal and are dedicated to building up each individual. Though deliberately limited in size, most are also dedicated to service beyond their own members. Strengthened in close community, the members individually and as a group live prophetically and practically in service to the community or to the world at large.

Much can be learned from this model, and many may choose to implement some form of a care, fellowship, "agape," or "discipleship" community. This is a basic structure that most certainly nurtures family and, when it is lived "in Christ," most certainly supports and nourishes its members toward greater wellness.

To be sure, it requires much time, commitment, energy, and exercise of talents. Because of this—and because it seems so radical to many—this model is often dismissed quickly or even feared. The risk of total community and total commitment frightens most of us. It doesn't help that we hear stories of tyranny and the strict control of members that is found in some communities. Jim Jones, Charles Manson, and the Moonies loom in our memories and even in our personal experiences.

Community "in Christ" can never be that. For practical or emotional reasons, we may not choose this model for ourselves, but we should first explore its strengths and step inside its boundaries in order to make our choice without simply reacting from fear.

Specially designed communities of care and fellowship within the context of the church are vital to our spiritual strength as a church and are indeed the most holistic. In some form, we as the church need to become communities of care.

Family Groupings Within Congregations

Family groupings within congregations are modified forms of more totally caring communities. Many larger churches in particular have found a renewed sense of community by dividing into smaller units of family groupings. In some cases this is done arbitrarily; in others it is managed by choice. Most often it is done partially by invitation. Each method has its advantages.

When the division is done arbitrarily, none are left out, groups are cross-sectional, and they usually fall into practical geographic locations. Whether all will truly be involved in these smaller groups of families usually depends on the leadership of each group.

When divided by choice, family groupings develop more naturally from common interests or out of common friendships. The obvious dangers are that cliques may form and that many will choose fringe involvement.

Organizing groups by invitation has the healthy benefit of allowing for choice and interest and thus usually shows more commitment. Without intentional encouragement, however, groups of families developed by choice may not represent cross sections of age, race, interest, economic level, or types of families and will certainly leave many of the hesitant out of the groups altogether.

Bringing groups of families together for any length of time generally provides primarily social and personal support. Worship in its more formal or traditional sense, education as a whole, and the service and mission of the church at large usually remain in the context of the whole community. Family groups may join together for fellowship, meals, Bible study, sharing of spiritual journeys, even for Communion, but the larger church community is the most central place and form for worship and education.

Joining several families together in groups sometimes fulfills the role of an extended family in communities with high mobility and high percentages of isolated family units. It is both good and necessary for our children to have grandparents, cousins, and aunts and uncles, and for our elderly to have grandchildren and sons and daughters. Family groupings can provide that in the context of the Christian community. The task of the family members in small groups is to know and to care for each other. This is usually worked out informally as members grow together in a smaller Christian community, guided and nurtured by the church of which they are also a part.

The model of family groupings is commonly an integral part of the formation of mission churches. It builds community by providing opportunities for open sharing and holistic fellowship.

In a transitory way, this model is very popular. "Cottage groups" are often temporarily designated for increasing fellowship, for exploring stewardship, or for sharing Lenten or Advent journeys. The church of which I am presently a member, for example, has a tradition of holding Lenten worship and discussion in cottage groups in private homes. Usually when Lent is over, the group disperses, but friendships that came out of such groups remain. Some of the closest friendships that came from those groups grew out of the multiage clusters. A group will be more holistic, more sensitive to each life stage, and more fully aware of each person's total life experience when whole family units are together, i.e., when children, parents, and grandparents learn and grow and share together.

Family groups may form for a variety of temporary reasons—camping, recreation, family learning experiences, retreats, etc. Joining together in small groups of families is an important supportive Christian experience that teaches us much about life and worship together in Christ, whether it be a temporary or a more permanent union. The most meaningful family groupings, however, require some extended period of time together to truly know and care for one another in ways that most effectively nurture and upbuild.

This is a practical model of life together that in many forms can encourage and nurture wellness to the degree that it remains openly and honestly and grace-fully in Christ.

Networking

Networking for growth and support can be structured into a church community both to meet needs of crisis and to encourage continued wellness, fullness, and community. Networking is simply providing channels or structures that connect people at points of interest and need.

My most common experience with networking is neighboring—knowing whom to ask for an extra egg, who might lend me a long extension ladder, who might want half of my zucchini, who needs a ride to the polls, who will lend me an ear when I am frustrated with my children, who would like to go for a walk with me, or who might know where I could find a particular tool or part. Networking is much more than finding out who will be willing to be of service to others. It is mutual connectedness of those who can offer service and those in need of service.

In a larger community, networking can be facilitated intentionally. Obviously, by myself I cannot know everything I would need to know about everyone in order to develop a network of all the members of my church. A simple form of networking, therefore, is dispersing information. Many congregations print a directory that lists not only the names and ages of each member (usually by household) but also general information of each member's choice. With this directory I can discover who enjoys cross-country skiing, who works or lives nearby, who likes to babysit, who has interests in common with me or my children, who is involved in particular social concerns, who understands learning disabilities, who is open to exchanging child care, and much more. A directory can tell me much that can lead to networking if I choose to participate. Usually it encourages a healthy degree of practical and social interrelatedness and interdependence.

Another simple form of networking is the formation of interest groups—printing information about, announcing, or signing people up for special interests. In this case, people join together to learn and share in mutual support. Adults may join in reading or study groups; families might get together for retreats; parents of teens might join for insight, learning, and support.

Networking can go much deeper and farther than this, however. Our greatest needs are the ones for which we are least likely to share or seek support within the context of groups organized merely around community fellowship and interest. There is only so much that I will reveal in the church directory; what I have most profoundly experienced is unlikely to be printed there. And I may not have the time or the self-assurance to go to an interest group; indeed, such groups may intimidate me at my points of greatest need.

To connect people at their points of greatest need, some congregations have successfully developed "friends programs." The premise is that each of us has had experiences that others are now going through and that therefore we might be a good friend to them in that common experience. Because I have dealt with my own infertility, for example, I might be able to help another in her struggle with the same—as a friend. Likewise, a couple who has lived the grief of crib death might be most supportive to a couple who recently experienced the same. A single parent might be a "friend" to another single parent.

All that is needed to network a "friends program" is the willingness of people to share their lives in friendship with others. Having received supportive friendship from others in our time of need, most of us are more than willing to do the same in turn. Networking thus is simply a matter of gathering and keeping information (confidentially, if requested) on those willing to befriend. Clergy then usually refer those in need or crisis to such "friends."

The breadth of human experience is a huge resource—children and adults who have come through divorce; adults who have lost a spouse or child by death; families who have lived through unemployment or sudden loss; men and women who have struggled with role expectations or through mid-life transitions; people who have been fired; teenagers who have lived with back braces; parents who have dealt with hyperactive children; people who have faced retirement; people with diabetes, epilepsy, or MS; parents whose children have joined cults or have gone into drugs; alcoholics; workaholics; people who have struggled with materialism—the list goes on and on. Any experience we have lived through can be a resource to another.

Congregations with a small number of "friends" volunteering often train them in the basics of sensitive listening and support. This can be helpful. Whole congregations can be sensitized as well, however. The model of "friends" has the further reward of increasing the congregation's resources as those who are befriended become willing and able to befriend in turn (an important principle of wellness explored in Chapter 3).

The scope of the linkages made in this program can be broader than person-to-person. We can learn a lot from the Jewish model of support when wartime casualties occurred. During World War II the Jewish community intentionally developed a model of crisis ministry to deal with news of war deaths. Step one was immediately to link the bereaved with their own support community for comfort and strength. We may be able to link people either with support groups of family or friends or, when that is neither possible nor preferable, with important community support groups.

Whether it is a one-to-one, family-to-family, or one-to-community situation, the goal of the "friends program" is the same—to empathetically befriend and strengthen a person in crisis or need so that he/she will grow and in turn be able to help others, for the needs go on endlessly in a community.

Another deeper form of networking is the development and availability of intentional support groups. More than mere interest groups, these usually open channels of deeper support, often provide educational insight, and enrich people in an interdependent relationship to family and others. To truly form a network, support groups need to continually reach out to draw in those in need as the ones once closely supported move on. Support groups often grow out of crises. Common groups are divorce adjustment groups, parents of teens in trouble, groups of recently widowed, parents of preschoolers, or families in unemployment. Though the group may continue, individual members usually move on.

Prayer chains are a form of networking. Groups traditionally operating in your congregation may also be forming networks to meet important needs. I have even had fellow choir members respond to me with concrete support and care in times of need. Much natural networking happens when people live in care and love for each other. The structure of a church can encourage this and broaden the scope and the depth of human interdependence and care. And again you will discover that networking done holistically—across generations and in the total family—carries the richest depth and blessing. Networking opens wells of common experiences and doors to resources within ourselves, in our own family and church community, and in the larger community "out there," which also has rich resources for wellness and care.

Expand Intentional Lay Ministry

A popular structure for increasing ministry to the family is to *expand intentional lay ministry* within a congregation. This might be done through a formal diaconate system, the appointment of lay ministers, a special training program for interested laity, or merely a loosely structured corps of volunteers. Leaders already appointed within the constitutional structure of the church may be equipped or sensitized for broader areas of lay ministry, for example.

The church has a long tradition of lay ministry by deacons and deaconesses. I remember a clear distinction between deacons and trustees in the rural church of my childhood. I remember also the active lay work of deaconesses in the Midwest. In restructuring churches we have, for the most part, merged both offices into a "church council" and "committees." We may have a "fellowship committee," but few diaconate systems remain.

What may have also disappeared, however, is the ministry task of the council and of the laity in general. And where "ministry" is considered, it is seen only in terms of service or mission to those outside the church. The task within the church is often merely the maintenance of the structure. Many congregations are rediscovering the service of lay ministry to the church as the body of Christ—ministry to each other, which strengthens us to be of service also to those outside.

I know of a congregation, for example, that rather carefully selects and trains several lay people whose task it is to know a small group of people, listen to them, and connect them with clergy and other resources when there is a need. These designated lay people themselves also participate in ongoing support and in-service education. I have seen other congregations train lay people in listening or friendship ministry to work both within the congregation and within their own community and job contexts. Usually there is some link with the pastor in this form also. In our community, for example, there is an ecumenical Befriender training program; congregations are using it to expand lay ministry to the family. In nine months of training, Befrienders are sensitized to their own spirituality and to common personal and social crises. Thus they learn how best to nurture, support, and listen to others—how to reach out to and befriend others. My husband and I once served as resources for a conference workshop on "Equipping the Saints." The intent was to better equip laity to listen and respond to those in their midst. Each denomination usually has its own training program for expanding lay ministry.

There is a growing sensitivity to broadening our ministry to the family by strengthening person-to-person ministry within congregations. Expanding intentional lay ministry seems to be a good place to begin. Depending on how many will serve and how comprehensive the structure is, *some* will be more cared for and nurtured toward wellness; I doubt that *all* will be reached in this structure so long as it is not comprehensive and is only a small piece of the church's ministry. Nevertheless, it is an important piece and a good beginning.

Expand Specific Family Ministry

A rather traditional church structure may increase ministry to family by intentionally *expanding specific family ministry*. This structure may appear to be no different than the church that is not particularly dedicated to nurturing family wellness in Christ. The danger is that indeed it may be no different. With this expanded structure we may become merely a church of programs, or worse yet, we may be encumbered with an overload of them. A traditional church that is expanding ministry to the family will typically increase family events, support groups, education opportunities sensitive to the life cycle, and enrichment opportunities for couples, for singles and for families. This is good. For this structure to work, however, it must pervade all traditional areas rather than simply add to what already exists. Worship, education, service, and mission can all be sensitive to family wellness. A mere shift from "adult services" held simultaneously with the Sunday school hour to a "family worship service" can be an expansion of family ministry. Service and mission done by multigenerational groups nurtures family wellness at the same time that service is rendered. The character of each separate function of the church shifts with a greater awareness of family wholeness. The most enjoyable church choirs in which I have sung (and not at all lacking in sound quality) were cross-generational. The lilt of a young voice adds much to the steady resonant tones of maturity. And I have learned much from children in education hours.

It is indeed possible to blend opportunities for full family and community participation into the traditional structures that are so reassuring for many of us. What is required here is a careful look at what we value most, a willingness to trade some rather traditional programs for others more sensitive to family wellness, and a flexibility in traditional forms that would make room for fuller family participation.

Alternative Structures

Radically nontraditional *alternative structures* dedicated to family wellness and fullness in Christ evolve out of an obvious need. From the beginning there is usually a strong commitment to be different from what now exists in order to be the caring body of Christ. People begin anew and build a form and structure that may not reflect any traditional mode but fits who they are. Thus the variety of alternative structures is broad. Worship forms and schedules, education forms, and very often service to the community may seem radically different from what most of us are used to.

Alternative communities of faith are often small and are usually alert to individual and community needs—at all ages. What they may lack in educational formality or organization they usually make up for in one-to-one adult concern for and relationship to each youth. Much community activity is multigenerational and linked with a broad spectrum of life (e.g., church members may garden together to help feed each family and to help feed the poor of the community or recreate together as a whole community in retreat, worship, and song or support each other in daily tasks of home and community upkeep and care).

Some of these are urban "store front" communities, dedicated to the mission of being with the surrounding urban family. They will be flexible and responsive to shifting needs. They may also work concretely toward family and community wellness when it is appropriate as a practical expression of life in Christ.

Some are community churches, located in smaller communities where separation by denomination seems far less important than community life lived together in Christ. These will often be centers of community for all ages.

Alternative forms can be excellent flexible structures for exciting creative family ministry. But they cannot be forced into existence. Without an obvious need, the energy to initiate such communities of faith is usually weak. In many cases, they are not even necessary. Where they are needed, they provide an essential form for building wellness and wholeness in the Christian community.

These six basic forms can be rural or urban, lie within the jurisdiction of many denominations, and represent a wide range of demography (churches predominantly young, predominantly German, predominantly black or white, predominantly elderly, etc.). To be wholly family, however, and to be dedicated to life together, they must not exclude by choice. Nor can they be strictly self-limited and claim dedication to God's family. To wake up to wholeness is to live and act in community beyond the walls of the church—to be in relationship with the whole created family of God.

To this end—to be the people of God—the variations and combinations of these forms take shape. All of these forms have worked well for some. All have probably failed somewhere for others. What makes a structure succeed is the ministry it conveys. The form is merely a medium and expression of the function—to be the people of God.

Look at the forms of God's people throughout Scripture. They change incredibly. They had to change to convey their true purpose. The people first grew in faith in patriarchal tribes. With careful rules and regulations they were led by Moses in the wilderness. To preserve their identity as people of Yahweh, they settled in the Promised Land, divided into tribes, and were ruled by judges; their task was not to mingle but to remain true to their covenant (Joshua 23 and 24:1-28). Later, fearing that Samuel's sons would no longer follow God's ways, the people formed a new structure under kings. Though their true motive may have been to be like other nations and to have kings for battle, God nevertheless worked out His purpose through that structure, too. Sending prophets to call His people back to the covenant, He preserved a remnant. Like a mother, God forgot not the people and nurtured them even in exile.

In the New Testament forms again change. No longer are God's people in tribes or kingdoms ruled by patriarchs. Jesus gathers disciples around Him in a family to be "fishers of men." Men and women alike (women and children were no longer considered property in the sight of Christ) lived in Christian community, often restructuring the families of their birth. Look at the radical form of Christian community in Acts—a form needed to preserve and testify to the faith:

> Now the company of those who believed were of one heart and soul, and no one said that any of the things which he possessed was his own, but they had everything in common. And with great power the apostles gave their testimony to the resurrection of the Lord Jesus, and great grace was upon them. There was not a needy person among them, for as many as were possessors of lands or houses sold them, and brought the proceeds of what was sold and laid it at the apostles' feet; and distribution was made to each as any had need. (Acts 4:32-35)
>
> And day by day, attending the temple together and breaking bread in their homes, they partook of food with glad and generous hearts, praising God and having favor with all the people. And the Lord added to their number day by day those who were being saved. (Acts 2:46-47)

Imagine the structure needed to "baptize all nations": two-by-two apostles went, supported by their larger family communities of faith. That is also what it was to be the people of God.

The communities of Paul's journeys had their emerging forms, too. Part of their mission was to be joined to each other in love and service. To be the people of God was to be united as the body of Christ, supporting each one in his/her gifts and united in love with kindness and patience (1 Cor. 12—13). They understood that

> speaking the truth in love, we are to grow up in every way into Him who is the Head, into Christ, from whom the whole body, joined and knit together by every joint with which it is supplied, when each part is working properly, makes bodily growth and upbuilds itself in love. (Eph. 4:15-16)

The whole community was to be dedicated to this family wholeness.

The form we choose as a community of faith comes from knowing who we are as the people of God. Our church has always reflected this. Changes have been made at different times to fit new circumstances—in order to upbuild our life in Christ. We need continually to choose, form, or grow in the structure that best fulfills our purpose in covenanted relationship with God. The structure will never be our sole reason for being a church. Church structure serves the function of living in Christ. How can we best live as the total body of Christ? How can we best nurture each one in the fullness of life in Christ, in wellness, and in wholeness?

Dare to be idealistic, and be realistic in that ideal. What forms of ministry best fulfill God's purpose in community, in family, for your particular congregation? What might realistically work? Where is this purpose now worked out and how might it be strengthened? None of our communities is a perfect model of Christian life or service, but all of us are the people of God.

7. *What of the Particulars—the Methods?*

What does specific ministry to the family look like? Very simply, ministry to the family is God's children mutually living out God's purpose for their lives. That purpose is life abundant as each one is called to wholeness, fullness, and service in Christ.

What forms does this ministry take? What methods does it use? How, in very specific ways, can we lead each other into wholeness, fullness, and service? How can we encourage care to everyone at all ages? What does specific ministry to the family look like?

Ministry to the family can be implemented in three basic modes: *support, education,* and *enrichment.* These modes have already been described; it might be helpful to define them more carefully and to look at how they are specifically carried out. Then as you explore familiar types of family programs, you will be able both to recognize each mode at work and to apply concrete methods to each familiar area of ministry.

Support

Support ministry can mean concrete support—offering food, money, transportation, physical care and labor, or helpful skills to those in need. Support can also mean providing emotional support. Ministries of support can be one-to-one ministries, mutual group support, or the linking of individuals or families to larger support systems. The formal one-to-one support most common to congregations is pastoral counseling. Much informal one-to-one support happens in friendships, and some is done in intentional programs of lay ministry. Primarily, one-to-one support is empathetic listening and care-full encouragement and confrontation—individual "invitations to growth."

Counseling support of an individual or a family, whether in formal therapy, pastoral counseling, or the counsel of a friend, offers a safe, trusting relationship. Within an accepting relationship, one is invited to express feelings and thoughts freely and is challenged and invited to face and cope with disturbing feelings, situations, or thoughts. A supportive counselor listens, reflects, empathizes, respects, and confronts. Christian therapy that recognizes each person in full faith-life dimensions is important support ministry.

Group support brings people together in common situations. A group may or may not have a leader. If leaderless, it usually involves sharing resources from each one's life experience. Such groups may form to support each member in a particular common life experience or to study books or other educational and inspirational material of common concern to all. Groups formed around a common task or interest sometimes become personal support groups even though that may not have been their original intent. Choirs, education committees, altar guilds, or sewing circles, for example, become support groups when members show true interest and care for each other. Support can also happen by coordination as much as by group process. Young mothers joining to exchange child care is a form of support in common experience.

Groups led by clergy, lay leaders, or professionals tend to have a more intentional focus. They might be more educational by choice or more intensely therapeutic (i.e., committed to each one's inner wellness and growth). Such groups usually have from 6 to 12 members and are not so much social as focused on individual growth. Because of their very purpose of supporting individuals or families during a time of crisis, transition, or need, they are seldom permanent (or at least do not have a permanent membership).

Linking individuals with larger support systems most often reaches beyond the congregation's private ministry. Putting alcoholics in contact with Alcoholics Anonymous, distressed or isolated parents with parent centers, and individuals or families in need of therapy with counseling centers is a good example of reaching beyond your congregation for support ministry. The very presence of a caring congregation can also provide families with a larger support system, however. My experience with funerals is like that. The funeral is a service that helps me to recognize that I am, indeed, not alone in my grief. There is a community that shares in it—and also shares my hope.

All of these support ministries work with a common understanding that support is a step toward wellness, not the end of the ministry. Support ministry in very specific and challenging terms needs to nurture people first toward independence and ultimately toward interdependence and service. It is sympathetic but not necessarily supportive to listen over and over again to an elderly woman bemoan the loss of her husband, her health, or her home. Support ministry will also challenge her toward new life, new hope, and new friends in her new environment. It is not supportive to repeatedly listen to the gripes and frustrations of a housebound mother of preschoolers. Support ministry will also challenge her to explore alternatives, make changes, and alter perspectives. To be in a Christian community does not mean forever leaning on other Christians. Support ministry in all its forms always aims toward growth. It is truly a ministry of upbuilding.

As we continue to build each other up in the faith, we will also continue to reach out to each other in healthy modes of interdependent support. This support—that of a brother or sister in Christ—is also part of intentional support ministry. This ministry reaches out in physical, emotional, and spiritual ways to those experiencing crisis, to those in need of empathy and strength, and to those living in continued interdependent Christian community with each other.

Education

Education as a mode of ministry has a long and varied history. In congregations it is usually a group or class ministry, but it sometimes also involves working with individuals, couples, or families (e.g., instruction in the faith, instruction for marriage, for joining the church, and the like). What education looks like in each congregation may be vastly different. I am going to describe what I see—and to propose a form that I find more conducive to learning.

Education is often described as pedagogic. Pedagogy, the art or science of teaching, suggests that there is important content or dogma to be taught—to be passed on as a body of knowledge. The emphasis of pedagogy is *teaching*—in some way providing others with knowledge. The teacher passes on the knowledge to the student. The teacher might tell stories (a delightful method of teaching), list facts, or explain material. It is then up to the student to remember the story, the fact, and the material. You probably recognize this form in your Sunday school, your adult education classes, your confirmation instruction, or even in the sermons you hear or deliver. I certainly recognize pedagogy in my own teaching experiences and style. The only time I am sorely uncomfortable with this form is when it becomes pedantic. However, I always wonder how much one really "learns" with this method. Pedagogy ensures teaching—and some entertaining, delightful, or impressive teaching at that—but that does not necessarily mean learning has happened.

Education in congregations usually takes the form of pedagogy. Material is taught. Differences in approach are usually only a matter of using various deductive or inductive methods. We might proceed by logic, beginning with what we know or firmly believe and going on to what we can logically deduce or reason out. Or we might begin with what we observe and finally proceed to what we can know or believe or induce (the scientific process). But we work with material, knowledge, ideas, and words, and we usually ask teachers to "teach us." Adult education is usually the knowledge or expertise of one person given or told to others. Adult Bible study usually involves reading some material and carefully looking step-by-step at what is read, thus hoping to understand what is meant by those written words; it is often a discussion of the text alone. Sunday school may involve reading some material and writing answers or talking about exactly what was read. Confirmation instruction may simply be teaching for memory the dogmas of the church and the facts of Biblical and church history. All of this is pedagogy. I remember much that was passed on to me pedagogically.

Learning is not the same as pedagogic education. In our education ministry, we must take this seriously. Were I to ask you what you learned in high school, for example, you might answer with more than was taught in the classroom. You might not mention anything that came out of textbooks! Were I to ask you what you learned in Sunday school or confirmation class, I hope you would tell me Bible stories or recite the Creed, but I would not be surprised to hear, "I learned that the big words in the Bible are embarrassingly hard to pronounce," or "I learned that pastors and teachers hate it when you tilt your chair back." Learning is *knowing* a subject, a skill, a truth. We may not know by mere pedagogy. We learn when we are instructed, when we study, or when we experience—and *know* it for ourselves. Learning is changing something in our heads, our skills, our attitudes, or our habits. When a child says, "I learned to tie my shoe today," that child means, "I can tie my shoe," not "Daddy showed me how." I have been shown many things, told many things, and have studied many things that I still do not know. I have not learned.

Education needs to combine teaching and learning. Experiential education can do this. When we link ideas with our own experiences, or when we actually experience how ideas work, we invest ourselves in those ideas and are more likely to learn. A Bible study on the church as the body of Christ that allows for the sharing of people's experiences or that plunges into how each one experiences the body of Christ is somewhat experiential. If we can tap into images of the right brain (the creative, imaginative half of the brain), we can broaden the experience. What might the body of Christ look like in a picture, an image, a metaphor? Add a physical experience. Ask a group to "sculpt" the body of Christ (make a human sculpture by positioning themselves in some group configuration); explore what that feels like to each member. Then go back to the sharing, exploring, and rereading of the text. This is experiential education. Children and families exploring God's creation—actually moving out into nature, walking through swamplands, forest, or prairie as they study God's creative life in process and balance—is experiential. With the background of this experiential learning of God's intricate balance of nature, what learning would you expect when you then walk by polluted streams and eroded farmland? Experiential education is very conducive to learning, and learning leads to action. Many have heard or read about ecology. Those who have experienced the beauty of nature and its loss will act on what they have learned. Many have heard or read of the church community as the body of Christ. Those who have felt or yearned for its power and love will work to enact it.

The process of experiential education—and indeed it is a process, a continuing development—is really quite simple. Begin with each one's concrete experience—something remembered or shared by others or, better yet, something the person has actually done. Then draw learning out of the experience. What do you notice? What was it like? Talking about and drawing together feelings and ideas brings us to a more abstract level. Now we can look at, "teach," or study an abstract idea; each one is more invested in the idea and already understands its experience because we began with the concrete. After the abstract idea has been shared, go back to what was experienced. How is it or can it be acted out in concrete ways? How does it look when it is acted out?

Let's look at a specific and perhaps familiar example. Suppose I were asked to teach about God's desire that we "trust in Him." I might begin with a "trust walk." I might ask people to pair off and walk with each other, one blindfolded while the other serves as guide. Or I might ask one to fall backward into the arms of the other, keeping the body rigid and not looking back. After that experience, people could share what it was like for them. Then in small groups or triads we might begin to share experiences of trust that we have had in our lives. We might draw these feelings and reflections together as a large group and jot down what trust means to the group. Then I might ask the group to study particular Scripture passages that invite us to trust in God. Again, we might study in small groups and share our ideas in turn with the larger group. If I choose, I might add to the learnings and ideas that came out of the small group discussions by sharing abstract principles of faith or theology. I might then share a story of what trusting in God meant for a Bible character. It would be fun for them to draw pictures of Bible figures they recall who trusted in God or a group mural of "trust in God"—pictures with symbols of what it meant specifically for those who trusted in God or for those who refused such trust. Or it might be fun to roleplay these stories and then reflect on them. Finally, I would ask them to explore what trusting fully in God might mean for them right now in their lives.

The principle at work here is to move from concrete experience to the abstract and then to apply it back down to the realm of personal experience:

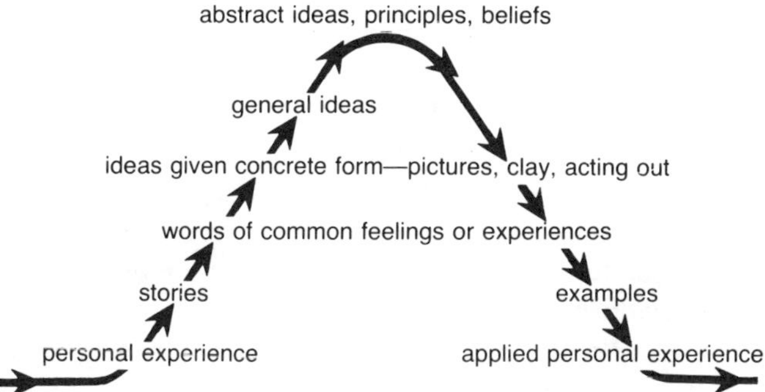

There is process and action in this structure. There is usually learning. The "teaching" involved is in the guiding of a process, in clearly and usually briefly explaining the abstract, and perhaps in developing a skill. The "learning" is in knowing the idea as one has experienced it and in seeing and acting on new possibilities that spring from that knowledge.

Another principle at work here is that education is most comprehensive and complete when it involves all of our modes of learning or receiving ideas and skills. We are basically auditory, kinesthetic, or visual—usually predominantly one of the three, but all three in total. To be sure, any group of people represents all three. Education that reaches all people in any group needs to include all three: visual (written words, pictures, graphs, objects, films), auditory (spoken words, verbal sharing, music, noises), and kinesthetic (physical experiences—walking through, touching, feeling, acting out). We also learn either with our left brain (basically the analytic) or our right brain (basically the imaginative). Both need to be engaged for us to fully "know." And we learn with our intellect, our emotions, and our bodies. Again, all three need to be engaged in total learning. I begin to understand stress, for example, when I become aware of how my body responds to stress, when I can identify emotions I experience with stress, and when I understand analytically and scientifically or can picture or explain a little bit about what stress is. I learn when I *know* my stress and can act on how it affects me.

One of the finest examples of education I have seen took place in a camp setting. Using a "ropes course," participants learned trust, support, creative self-reliance, cooperation, and a multitude of skills of endurance and interrelatedness. In small groups participants were taken through a complicated and difficult obstacle course, impossible for any one individual to complete alone. The only way to survive in this imaginative course of potential disasters was to pull together as a group, drawing on creative and even far-out suggestions from the group and using all the physical and mental resources of the group. This, coupled with a week in Christian community, was for many a powerful learning experience that went far beyond what could have been taught with the more traditional methods of a Bible camp, particularly for a group of inner-city youth. Learning happened in experiences of mind, body, and emotion, in engaging both imagination and reason, and in working at all levels of the concrete and the abstract.

It is important for those who work in the education ministry of our congregations to be sensitive to and familiar with this principle of complete education.

Enrichment

Enrichment—at least as a term—is a new mode of ministry for many. In specific programming it is primarily a structured opportunity for growth. The premise, as you may recall, is that each of us has untapped potential. Enrichment ministry is usually carried out in recreation and retreat programs, in opportunities for worship and meditation, or in structured opportunities for spiritual growth (e.g., reading circles, Bible studies). The real content of enrichment programs is what is within each participant. It is typical—and a good idea—to combine enrichment with education and to add some skill or content, but enrichment in itself is simply providing an opportunity for something to happen.

The structure of enrichment programs, then, is simply that—structure—and it dare not be "overstructure" or it will squelch the very spontaneity that encourages growth. A specific and truly valuable example, which will be explained in more detail later, is the marriage retreat, a structured opportunity for couples to spend time together apart from their routine tasks, jobs, and responsibilities. Youth camps are also often enrichment programs.

Most enrichment programs are relational. That is, they are structured opportunities for relating in new ways to others, to one another, to God, or to ourselves. When we relate in new ways, we discover new things about ourselves—and we grow. When I participate in a family camp where I play, learn, try new things, worship, sing, and work with my husband and my children in ways different from the routine, I discover and appreciate and grow. When I set aside an evening with my husband to attend a provocative play and to share our thoughts over a cup of coffee or during a walk along the lake, I am enriched in our relationship—new possibilities and new growth can emerge. When I set aside a time for daily meditation and disciplined exercise and relaxation, I grow in my relationship to God and to myself.

Enrichment programs are not just "hanging around" together, time off, or a chance to talk. They are intentionally structured to put us into new situations from which learning and growing will emerge. Enrichment can happen without this, but it is important in planning enrichment programs to provide opportunities for growth.

Specific programs of ministry to the family will come in modes of support, education, or enrichment—or combinations of the three.

I have given most space and attention to the education mode. Support ministry is best described by those who counsel, and I urge you to seek particulars from them. Enrichment is both new and nebulous as a recognized form; time and growth in this mode will teach its particulars. But the education mode deserves emphasis for reasons other than my professional inclinations or experience. In many ways, education blends all three modes, offering support and enrichment in the context of learning. Education is also a mode easily implemented in institutions and therefore has been most popular to date in most churches. Yet each of the three, separately or as combined modes, needs deliberate attention.

Specific programs will also come in categories of age and interest. The interest categories explain themselves and usually follow lines of common experience (e.g., parents groups, reading circles, singles groups). Age categories are familiar to us all: nursery/preschool, elementary age, junior high, teenage or high school age, college age, young adult (very broad), mid-life (a rather new one that means 35—45 as a rule), retirement age, and elderly.

Two other categories are important in family life ministry: multi-aged and cross-generational. Multi-aged can mean grades 1—8, K—12, or all ages. Multi-aged Sunday school classes usually involve children (grades K—6, 1—8, K—12, etc.). Multi-aged canoe trips usually means trips that are open to all ages. Cross-generational, on the other hand, means an intentional mixing of generations—parents and children, for example. Cross-generational may also mean the spanning of all generations, from the infant to the elderly.

These new age categories are more than definitions. In the mixing of ages we learn from each other. Ours is both the wisdom of children and of the aged. We need the learning, the joy, and the care that comes from a multi-aged community. We need the belonging to community that spans all generations.

Grouping by age or by interest is a practical method of programming. In so doing, choose groupings that fit not only convenience or tradition. Groupings must provide the learning or support that is most needed in each situation. Celebrating the Nativity is a total community event, spanning all ages and interests. Likewise, living and learning the way of Christ must sometimes be in total community. On the other hand, growing into fuller parenting might happen most effectively in the supportive context of a group of parents, at least for a while. Groupings are merely forms we choose to fit best what we see as our function or purpose in each learning situation.

With these definitions, methods, and categories in mind, we can now look at typical family life programs.

8. Typical Family Programs

Family ministry is knowing and caring for each other as brothers and sisters in Christ. This can be done informally, but it needs to be done concretely. It can be done formally in programs that begin and encourage the mutual ministry of love. Recognizing that programs can just as easily hinder true ministry, most of us nevertheless need them to make the ministries to which we are firmly dedicated concrete and specific.

By now you have formed images of principles, possibilities, and even basic structures, but what of the particular programs? In the very process of exploring, you have probably already begun to see the particulars for your congregation. Yet it is helpful to look at specific possibilities. I therefore share what particular programs in family ministry might look like. None of these is a total family ministry in itself. All of them have somewhere at sometime been an important part of ministry to the family.

Wholeness Programs for Individuals

Wholeness or wellness programs for individuals may seem to contradict all we have said about the family as involving interpersonal life together. It is not at all out of place, however, when we consider the direction in which solitude and meditation will take us. And it is not out of place when we recognize that intimacy and relationship with another come from first knowing oneself.

The discovery that "no man is an island," that all of humanity is one, that I am indeed my brother's keeper comes from the wells of solitude and meditation. As a monk, Meister Eckhardt learned from the heart the ever-cycling creative energy of life that is tapped in human potential for compassion and care. To be spiritual is always to be alive to all that is alive. Thomas Merton in solitary meditation discovered his unity with humanity. By going inside himself, he discovered not the center of the universe but part of a larger whole. Meditation—openness to God and to one's inner self—is not self-centered; rather, it tunes us into our very centeredness in God and to our unity with others—with all the family of God. Henri Nouwen, in meditation and solitude, discovered an inevitable openness to others. He recognized that we must first learn solitude; then we can truly learn hospitality.

Paul's prayer for all families is likewise a prayer of meditation:

> For this reason I bow my knees before the Father, from whom every family in heaven and on earth is named, that according to the riches of His glory He may grant you to be strengthened with might through His Spirit in the inner man, and that Christ may dwell in your hearts through faith; that you, being rooted and grounded in love, may have power to comprehend with all the saints what is the breadth and length and height and depth, and to know the love of Christ which surpasses knowledge, that you may be filled with all the fullness of God. (Eph. 3:14-19)

Encouraging, supporting, and structuring meditation is part of family life ministry; many congregations include this in their overall program.

I previously discussed the need for "stress ministry." Personal wholeness and wellness, knowing and accepting oneself, is near the center of stress ministry. At its core is our very belief system, a belief we must dare to discover in relationship to ourselves, our faith, and our God—in spiritual meditation.

Programs for coping with stress come in many forms. We might work simply at the center to strengthen our faith. We might work on knowing and accepting ourselves, learning ways of self-esteem and self-discovery. Or we might program ways to help people cope with stress—ways of relaxation, of gaining more strength, support, and control in our lives, of knowing and asserting ourselves. All of these are important in stress ministry and might be introduced in an initial workshop on stress. Some awareness of stress—how we experience it, what "stressors" are and with what attitude we receive them, what physical and emotional process is at work in stress, and what can be done about stress—can be a helpful foundation for ongoing programs on managing stress.

Personal wholeness means wholeness of spirit, mind, and body. Therefore, programs on sexuality and physical and emotional health are a part of family life ministry. We are created with a body by a God who chose to reveal Himself incarnate. Surely our physical response and celebration is a part of our life "in Christ," and "embodied" we live in family. Being comfortable with our sexuality, we can be responsible and free in our physical relationship with others.

Personal wellness workshops and programs might also typically deal with such issues as grief, death and dying, or personal mid-life crises—critical issues of faith in daily life.

In communities where such needs are not already being met effectively, ministry as health, nutrition, and exercise might be a part of ministry toward personal wellness. We are called to clothe the naked and feed the hungry (Matt. 25). I have seen literacy and language study become a part of Christian ministry toward personal growth.

All of the above possibilities are part of family ministry since they move each person into wholeness in Christ and often into more comfortable relationships with others.

Family Workshops

Family workshops are an increasingly typical form of family ministry. At first glance this might seem to be exclusive, but it need not be. In designing family programs, "family" can be defined as broadly as you wish.

Some family programs are total church-family events—multi-aged and cross-generational. These events are usually designed to bring the church together as a family to celebrate and share life. They might center on a task such as cleaning the church grounds or on an event such as a "social," a musical, or a fair. They might focus on a Christ event, such as Palm Sunday or the Nativity. Faith events are also opportunities for church-family programs: All Saints' Day, Confirmation, World Day of Prayer.

Family programs for households need not be exclusive either. Our "primary family" is those people closest to us in a primary caring and nurturing relationship. Few of us lack family in this sense. People coming together to understand and explore their unique family life can include all types of families. Single-parent families, "blended" or "step-families," two-parent families with children at home, childless couples, couples whose children have left home already—all of these families share common dynamics. Family workshops can bring them together.

Typical topics for these invariably fun workshops are (1) the family as a system, (2) understanding the dynamics of family living—how we get things done and how we are together, (3) family communication, (4) growing up in family (at all ages), (5) family cooperation, (6) family fun, and (7) family retreat. Less typical are topics like "families in crisis" and "family sexuality" (though not less typical as topics for teen workshops). These last two usually require some special resources or expertise but are just as central to family living.

What all family workshops share in common is doing things, learning, and having fun together. A family workshop is not segregated by age; all learn together, adults and youth in the same group. For this to happen successfully, family programs need to be active and involving. The rather popular family program format of a film, therefore, is hardly what I would call a "family workshop." This is a public viewing for all ages, some of whom happen to come as families. For a film to be a family program, a discussion needs to follow at the very least, and preferably ideas from the film would be explored and tried out in some active relational way. Process and experiential education is a very helpful guide in planning family workshops.

Family workshops focused on life together as primary units work for family household groups; family units that all live together are the natural learning groups when small groups are a part of the learning process. Families can be grouped together like this even within the Sunday morning format. As a part of Christian education, families can study God's creation together, learn more about the poor and the needy, or explore Christ's peace on earth. When groups study together as families, there is often a greater common commitment and impetus to do something together. Motivated by the love of Christ to feed the hungry, a family in our congregation, for example, regularly eats a weekly meal of rice and donates the cost saved on that meal to hunger appeals. Motivated to take part in a similar family activity, our children at the ages of five and seven joined us in a CROP hike. Together the four of us could walk over 20 miles for pledges.

Family workshops often build unity and mutual appreciation. This is a rewarding form of ministry with broad and exciting potential.

Parenting Classes

Because we are concerned about raising our children in the faith, *parenting classes or workshops* are also increasingly popular and are distinctly different from family workshops. The topic is obviously an issue of family life, but the target audience is much narrower. Parenting classes are for adults, particularly for adults with children under 18 years of age.

Because of the wide variation in issues at each age of child development, parenting classes are usually further divided into sections on planning for parenting, parents of preschoolers (unfortunately usually just "moms-and-tots" or mothers of preschoolers), parents of elementary age children, and the increasingly anxious parents of teens. Classes, support groups, or workshops are then usually designed to help parents better understand Christian parenting and coping with children at each age.

The parent-child relationship is an important part of the community of faith. Congregations that recognize this are able to design programs that do more than suggest "How to Discipline" or "How to Cope." Neither of these is the point of parenting. Children are also part of the body of Christ; they are not ours but God's. The goal of discipline is not to "keep them in line" according to our rules; Christian discipline is to guide and teach faithful responsibility:

> Hear, O Israel: the Lord our God is one Lord; and you shall love the Lord your God with all your heart, and with all your soul, and with all your might. And these words which I command you this day shall be upon your heart; and you shall teach them diligently to your children. (Deut. 6:4-7)

The parent-child relationship is a family relationship in Christ (Col. 3:12-17).

In this context, communication, a popular topic of parenting classes, is not merely a matter of getting your point across. Communication is rather sharing one's faith, upbuilding each other—and particularly nurturing and supporting our children. Paul's words apply as much to parenting as they do anywhere else in the Christian community: "Let no evil talk come out of your mouths, but only such as is good for edifying, as fits the occasion, that it may impart grace to those who hear" (Eph. 4:29).

The most effective parenting classes are those that explore, share, practice, and imagine new possibilities of parenting in the context of family unity in Christ and of each one's individual calling in Christ (our children's as well as our own). Prescriptions for the "Christian family" are out there for us to latch onto in parenting programs, but there is risk. They can be filled with stereotypes and restrictions. Parenting is part of our journey of faith and as such is our call. Built on solid principles of faith and psychology, parenting classes that create opportunities for learning new skills and help us become more aware of our child's development and of the dynamics of the parent-child relationship can open us up to exploring our unique parental relationship; they invite us to grow in wellness and wholeness in Christ in a way that is appropriate for us and our family.

The situation of the single parent is often set aside as a special area for family ministry. To some extent this is a good idea. The structure of a single-parent home is different, and the relationship between child and parent has some unique dynamics. Congregations that implement this specific form often join with other area groups or congregations in this ministry because of the typically limited size of such groups within any one parish. This limit in size is probably changing. And although being a single parent is unique, single parents also belong in community with all other parents—with a clear appreciation of their differences.

Parent-Teen Programs

Parent-teen (or parent-child) *programs* are more family workshops than parenting classes. Parents and teens come together either on topics of major concern or to understand more clearly the nature of their relationship lived in Christ. Younger or older siblings are not a part of these workshops; thus they are not truly family workshops.

Most parent-teen workshops focus in some way on communication—either the skill of sharing and listening itself or communicating about faith journeys, values, or issues of concern. Talk about communication is obviously no substitute for the real thing. Most communication workshops, therefore, get parents and teens into actual communicating—actively listening to each other and sharing feelings, thoughts, and wants in a safe environment of support and care. Skills might be taught, insights shared, and principles of healthy relating explored and modeled. Roleplaying is often an effective medium for this age group (particularly insightful when adults play teens and vice versa).

Programs in which parents and teens work and play together are also quite common. Parent-teen canoe trips and parent-teen car washes are good examples. More often, however, these are adult-teen activities rather than limited to teens with their actual parents.

Premarital Programs

Premarital workshops and instruction are part of a congregation's church-family ministry. In many parishes this may be viewed more as the pastor's ministry than the congregation's. Even when the instruction is handled privately and only by the pastor, it is nevertheless a congregational ministry.

With a growing awareness of divorce statistics and a seeming lack of covenant and commitment in the marriage relationship, this form of ministry is receiving more attention. Premarriage instruction is acknowledged as more than simply preparation for the wedding service. Preparing for the commitment of a life together in Christ is to be taken seriously. Couples are often asked to explore their communication patterns, their methods of resolving conflict, the patterns and attitudes that come from their families, their personal goals and shared values, and their patterns and needs in sexual and emotional intimacy.

To do this most efficiently and in many ways more effectively, many congregations in mainline denominations require that couples planning marriage attend workshops designed to explore these issues. Obviously, individual congregations may not have the resources or the regular number of couples to run such workshops. Therefore, if the larger church body does not provide such a resource itself, congregations often contract church social service agencies to offer regular workshops in cooperative area ministries.

Where these cooperative resources are not available, family ministry to premarrieds is still possible. Excellent materials for evaluation and instruction are available to aid the pastor in this congregational ministry.

Marriage Programs

Marriage programs come in a wide variety. Most common, perhaps, is the marriage retreat. A day, an overnight, or a weekend gives couples an opportunity to learn and to share. Retreats are times of enrichment and learning. Usually they are structured to give couples comfortable time together. (I always balk when I hear of a retreat scheduled at a site with bunk beds!) Usually some new insights (experiential education, I would hope) and worship are also part of the program.

Marriage support groups and marriage classes are the other most common forms. Support groups often develop from grass-roots interest or over semistructured topics, such as the discussion of a book or a set of tapes on marriage. Marriage classes are more intentional and educational. Basic skills and concepts are usually taught, explored, and practiced. Often outside resources are brought in. (This can give the clergy couple the opportunity of being one of the participating couples.) In the context of the church, classes on marriage can be important opportunities to share with others and to explore for oneself the meaning of daily living in grace and forgiveness in a covenant relationship in Christ.

Marriage programs might also be issue-oriented: the two-income marriage, sexuality, communication, male and female roles, budgeting and stewardship in marriage, for example. A lot of these are typically dealt with in brief one-hour programs with a speaker. As long as couples really go on to explore the issue, they can be effective. Remember that hearing about something hardly guarantees learning, however. Ministry—mutual service to each other—might demand more.

The value of all marriage programs is their support and recognition of marriage as living the new life in Christ—together. To recognize daily marriage as a way of life and a call to commitment and grace is to recognize the need for Christian ministry within marriage. The popularity and importance of the marriage retreat lies in an awareness of marriage as a daily liturgy of faith. Daily we invoke the name of God and of our beloved; in open and honest communication, in sharing and listening, we can experience daily confession and absolution; in acknowledging our shared histories in Christ and God's presence in our lives, we hear the Word and confess our faith; and in daily expressions of love we live in the benediction of God's grace. To live in fuller awareness of this life in Christ, chosen and covenanted to each other, we need the support, learning, and enrichment of marriage programs.

Singles Ministry

Singles ministry seems a strange form to include in family ministry. If I were to suggest one important form of singles ministry, it would be to validate and recognize singles as individuals within the family of God. Singles do not pretend to be other than singles. Sometimes in our "family" ministry we try to make everyone units of a family first. Then, of course, we can more easily fit them into family ministry. "Bring your family!" This has to be uncomfortable for the single person who chooses to live alone. And such an invitation can be especially painful for the single who lives alone because of loss. There is room for the single—alone—in the family of God. Singles, as singles, are a part of the church-family without having to link with another family unit in order to belong. Invitations like, "ALL are welcome,'' ''a multigenerational event,'' and ''join the church-family'' encourage the single to join with other members in family events of learning and fun.

A specific singles ministry invites singles to join with each other in areas of growth and common concern. Unless the group so chooses, be careful not to make matchmaking the intent of these groups. Then the message again would be, ''It's not OK to be single.'' Single life is a unique way of life, and singles often look to other singles for support in that life-style. A singles ministry can intentionally provide opportunity for that support. In particular, single parents express that need. Like other interest groups, however, singles groups need to be acknowledged as part of a larger whole—the family of God in a particular community.

There is another area of singles ministry that is primarily a service ministry. Single parents who are struggling economically or cut off from past friends and family sometimes especially need services that we can coordinate or provide. This is true also of single older adults. Again, the best support involves mutual coordination and self-help whenever possible. This is as much a ministry of education and enrichment as it is of actual physical support.

For most congregations singles ministry is a relatively new form. The most successful singles ministries have often gone beyond the membership of an individual church. In some cases, an effective singles ministry increases the singles membership in congregations that are expressly open to them. The shape of this ministry needs to come from singles themselves and to rise out of the context in which singles find themselves in each particular community.

Life Stage Ministry

Life stage/life events ministry broadly defines most other forms common to family life programming.

Much of what has long been a traditional part of church ministry falls into this category: Sunday school education, youth ministry, confirmation. That barely scratches the surface of total life experience, however. From birth till death there is need and opportunity for ministry. Furthermore, in these traditional ministries we sometimes pull youth out of the family to instruct and work with them. Recognizing that they are a part of family ministry helps us keep them in the context of family.

Confirmation instruction, for example, in the most holistic sense can and should be a family ministry. Parents must be involved in this journey of faith. Structuring opportunities for parents and teens to share in it can be a part of the instruction. Communication between parent and teen is a key element in the journey, and ultimately the confirmation vows are a family event of transition, reaffirmation, and acknowledged autonomy—all essential to healthy teen transition to adulthood. The Jewish *Bar Mitzvah* is such a holistic event, a celebrated life transition rich in family and religious blessing.

Sunday school is also very much a part of family ministry—much more than a place to "drop the kids." To help appreciate this, many congregations are now trying occasional forms of cross-generational Sunday school as part of their regular curriculum, occasionally bringing parents and children together to study and celebrate. In an Advent series of this kind, we as a family discovered our histories, the way the Messiah comes to us in our daily lives, and our hopes in faith as we together made a family wreath rich with symbols of family Christmas tradition and of Christ's presence in our lives. Together we learned and celebrated as we read Advent texts, sang Advent songs, and shared in a common task. And in the end we had an unusual Advent wreath that celebrated our uniqueness as a family and reminded us of the Advent of Christ in our lives.

Life stage family ministry needs to go beyond youth and beyond what we might segment as "spiritual training." If God is active in our total life history, then all of that history is a part of our ministry, and all that we experience is "holy"—i.e., dedicated to God. This means that vocational decisions, dating, our sexuality throughout our lives, parenting, mid-life, retirement, old age—every conceivable stage in life is lived in relationship to God and is a context for ministry to each other. Some life stages are difficult; Christian therapy, growth, and support groups can nurture us through these. Some are exciting; we can celebrate these together in faith. Some are frightening; we can guide each other through these. Support, education, and enrichment are needed throughout our life cycle.

Many critical life events and life stage transitions are touched in pastoral ministry. But no one pastor or even a staff of clergy could ever cover all of it. Here is an opportunity for expanded lay ministry—one-to-one befriending, individual care, and total family support.

Some life events are extreme and unique—events that need the caring response of one-to-one love, concern, and support. Others, though individual, are more common to all. We can minister to people in such events in support groups, larger groups of study and sharing, or education/enrichment classes for those closest to the event. Events like marriage, divorce, the death of a spouse, a death in the family, and the care of elderly parents are some examples.

Ministry in life stages and events needs to span all ages and all of life, for where God is active and present, we are there together in ministry in God's purpose.

Service Ministry

In the midst of these typical forms of church-family ministry we are also carrying out *service ministry* beyond ourselves. This is also an integral part of family ministry. All of humanity and all of creation is a part of God's family. Intentionally reaching out to the poor and oppressed is part of what it means to be our brother's keeper. Working for peace and justice and for wellness for all is essential to our universal life together in family. Living in responsible harmony with nature is part of our family wellness on earth.

Service ministry is often managed through task forces or other temporary forms of ministry. In times of obvious immediate need or concern, congregations might activate a special structure—for example, in response to high unemployment, refugee resettlement needs, or natural disasters. Much service ministry is done by joining forces with area church social service agencies. Foster care or drug treatment programs are good examples of this. Much is also done by working with national and worldwide organizations: Bread for the World, CROP, Project Hope, Lutheran World Relief. Other service ministry remains an ongoing concern of a congregation: the ecological balance of God's creation, justice within one's community, etc. In all forms, service ministry can be much more than money. We can alert all ages to our responsible relationship to all of God's family—and much of this can be done in actual tasks and in multigenerational modes.

These typical forms of programming church-family ministry should suggest particular possibilities for your congregation. Obviously, they are comprehensive. It would seem that everything is "family ministry." In some sense it is. A segmented notion of ministry often separates us from our brothers and sisters in Christ and keeps us from seeing our relatedness to all. We do not all need to serve on a task force for peace and justice, but we do all need to realize our family relationship with those who are suffering from war and oppression. We do not always need to meet with children and adults at the same time, but we do need to recognize people of all ages as brothers and sisters in Christ. We do not always need to concern ourselves with the "family" element of Sunday school and worship, but we need always to be aware that in these structures we are living, teaching, and celebrating our faith in a family relationship.

Ministry to the family pervades all dimensions of community life in Christ. A fuller understanding of family ministry will affect all areas of parish activity. For family ministry is the combining of faith and experience, theology and life event. It is an attitude of validating and caring for each in his/her own age and space as one of God's family. These programs are merely concrete expressions of that attitude, programs that nurture the abundant life to which each is called.

All of these typical programs are possible within the walls of one church. Most of them also encourage joining at times with other congregations or community groups in broadening and strengthening each particular ministry. And implementing some of them will require linking with resources outside the local church—resources of the church body, the community, and social service agencies. To go outside one's congregation for resources, however, is not to "give up" or "hand over" a ministry. It is rather to join as partners in a ministry of concern to both the local church and the broader community, a congregational ministry that is joined by others in Christian and human service.

What does specific ministry to family look like?

> So that we may no longer be children, tossed to and fro and carried about with every wind of doctrine, by the cunning of men, by their craftiness in deceitful wiles. Rather, speaking the truth in love, we are to grow up in every way into Him who is the Head, into Christ, from whom the whole body, joined and knit together by every joint with which it is supplied, when each part is working properly, makes bodily growth and upbuilds itself in love. (Eph. 4:14-16)

Ministry to the family is such upbuilding of each within primary and congregational units of family. It is for us to discover our function as individuals and congregations as we reflect on and respond to the love of Christ, which has reconciled us to God and called us into community. As we fulfill this function, each within our midst can in turn "grow up in every way into Christ." This is church family ministry lived out in concrete terms.

9. How Will Families Respond?

We are builders. We are dreamers. We see visions and possibilities. We are people of promise, people of hope, people of God's creation and creativity. Spanning all generations, we are founders and fledglings of family—the family of man, the family of God. We are gregarious creatures of love and of fear.

We fear. We fear change. We fear touching and being touched. We fear growth and responsibility. We fear rejection, hurt, and failure. We fear union with others and knowledge of ourselves. We are people with the pain of history and the disillusion of disappointment. We dare not try; we dare not dream.

We seek security. We seek stability. So we are creatures of habit. We are men, women, and children of set patterns and traditions.

Will we build visions that never materialize? Will we dream dreams that others never understand? Will we imagine, only to hold back?

If we or a few imagine and pour effort and plans into forms of our visions, will others receive and join with us in healing and upbuilding? How will families respond to notions of union and actions of care? Will the families we know around us be open to new forms of family ministry? How will our families respond?

I am surprised at how quickly doubt can cloud our visions. In the middle of writing the manuscript for this book, we made a major move, uprooting me from family, friends, neighborhood, and community. Weeks after the move I already doubted my goal. I seemed to have lost the context of family—in a community of strangers, in a new and unfamiliar church, without daily involvement in family life education, and alone most of the day. What did I know about family and community? How could I write of what I no longer experienced? What could I say that really mattered? What could I effect, envision, or build? What I penned seemed dull and without energy, without integrity, an image of shallow dreams and a shaky vision from the past. Domestic adjustment and half-empty cardboard boxes were what I was really all about. My young son saw my depression and overheard my doubts as I shared them with my spouse. He paused with swollen lip in the middle of his stumbling cornet practice; with motherly sentiment, I asked if a hug would help. "Don't need one," he said, "but I'll give you one. It might help your writing." Then with an impish grin and the wisdom and daring of his youth, he challenged, "If you don't believe in yourself, how can you write?"

I do believe in myself, and I believe in family. And the hug did help. In spite of all doubts and fears, the image of Christian community was still alive within me. What had I expected? Had I forgotten the turmoils, the ups and downs of moving? Had I expected to write without hesitancy, without adjustment—to write smoothly through the major upheaval of our whole family system, exciting as it might have been? Drawing reality into perspective helped me readjust my expectations and repossess my dream.

Knowing what to expect and reminding ourselves of the natural realities can help us follow through and build on our early visions of ministry. Knowing what to expect can indeed strengthen our ministry, which, after all, needs to be one of response and reality, not of private image and illusion.

When we venture into notions and forms of church-family ministry, what can we expect?

Allow me to share the reactions of a few who seem to me quite typical:

Bob and Elaine are a rather typical couple. Most would call their marriage "good." They were married young, just after Bob graduated from college. Elaine was eager to leave school after her sophomore year, not having settled on a major yet anyway. Marrying Bob seemed an exciting adventure compared to two more years of term papers and final exams. If she wanted to, she could always return to school later when she would know for sure what she wanted to do. And she was in love. Her parents had certainly not objected.

They liked Bob and had always assumed that Elaine would eventually marry and raise a family. It all fell into place for Bob, too, whose college years had gone as planned. Not only had he gone through school on an athletic scholarship; he had the luck of also getting into a business program just suited for moving into his father's business. Marrying Elaine fit into his plans. They had met late in his junior year, and there was no doubt in his mind that she would make the perfect wife.

Some years of their marriage had been hard. Elly was born just a year after the wedding, making the first year as filled with morning sickness, restrictions, and irritability as with the delights of young love. The years with preschoolers had been hard for both of them. Bob ended up investing most of his time in the business to avoid the domestic hassles. There was a year when Bob seemed muddled with the frustration of working with his father and the year that Elaine seemed depressed and irritated with the children. In times like those, they stayed clear of each other, and time moved them into better years—years of building a home together, building friendships, and enjoying the children. Marriage wasn't quite what either had expected, perhaps, but most anniversaries seemed worth celebrating.

After 16 years of marriage, Bob has "made it" in business. With the frustrating years of working with his father in the past, he is now running the business and must be quite satisfied, Elaine suspects. All the time and energy invested in the business has paid off. Elaine at 36 is still attractive and, with her delightful sociability, is an asset to his business, Bob reflects. One might suspect that they don't spend a lot of time together and maybe don't know a whole lot about each other. Elaine admits her doubts that Bob has ever understood her, and Bob assumes there is no need for Elaine to understand his world. They share the family. Here they can make reasonable decisions together if necessary, but for the most part, Elaine manages that quite well on her own.

Their daughter Elly is indeed a beauty; at 15 she already has a growing number of interested boyfriends. Bob worries about her sometimes; she seems moody and especially hot-tempered with her mother. But she spends a lot of time with her friends, and that makes things more pleasant at home.

Her brother Steve is affable and certainly easier to figure out, both parents would agree. His ambitions and investments already show up in his growing shelf of minor athletic trophies. At 12 he is doing well in school and is a delight to most of his proud relatives.

In the light of that, his stubborn independence is nothing to worry about.

Robby, the baby, is still young enough to be cute and lovable—and one might suspect he knows it. Steve and Elly call him a pest, complaining that he never leaves them alone and gets into their things even when they tell him otherwise. It is their job to watch him after school until Elaine comes home from classes. It is normal that they would complain.

Elaine has recently gone back to school. Finding any time for herself seemed impossible when the children were young. Now that Robby is in school, she figures she can finish her undergraduate degree in teaching. Before Robby was born, she had worked as a teacher's aid in the local grade school. Three years of working with second graders piqued her interest in teaching. Bob doesn't really understand. She doesn't need to work. He provides well for her. She has a beautiful home that they built after Robby was born. She can always find friends to shop or golf with. He doesn't mind if she does a little volunteer work here and there, but going back to school seems a waste of time. Elaine studies when he is not around.

They seem to get along well enough. Nothing serious has ever gone wrong in their marriage, it would seem. They have a fine home, three beautiful, healthy children, a lovely house, and plenty of friends. They are well-liked and respected in the community and the church. Elaine sometimes feels distant from Bob but certainly not enough to consider separation. All in all, they are a happy couple and live pretty predictable if not comfortable lives.

Elaine's mother moved to town after her husband passed away. Now that she lives nearby, she notices more about Elaine's marriage. She was happy to see that they had a "good marriage," not like her sister's children, who were now on the verge of a bitter divorce. She is pleased that she is welcome at Elaine's anytime and stops in daily, half out of interest and half out of her own loneliness. Elaine seems to be alone with their youngest a lot, too. Her mother appreciates that she can help out by watching Robby to relieve Elaine in her busy schedule. Now *they* are her family. As a member of the family, it is also apparent to her that things are not always comfortable or fun between Bob and Elaine. The occasional tension between Elly and Elaine and the irritation little Robby seems to arouse adds to the general discomfort of the home atmosphere. In spite of her loneliness, Mom stays away at these times.

The one place where Elaine's mother has always felt welcome is in the church. Here she has found a group of friends who have much in common. Most are also widows, and many see little of their families. It isn't the same as being with Elaine's family, of course—she misses the time with the children. But it fills the hours, and she much needs their comfortable companionship. Maybe because of her friends, she follows what happens at church more closely than does Elaine.

By now you surely see much in this family that warrants enrichment. Yet how will they respond to invitations to family ministry?

Elaine's mother wasn't much involved in the discussions or planning that led up to it, but she did notice that there was a growing interest in family activities in the church. Maybe this was partly why she began to pay closer attention to Elaine's family. Hoping to interest and support more families, the church now scheduled a series of classes or workshops for families. It looked fun and interesting to Elaine's mother. Maybe it was just what Bob and Elaine needed!

Elaine's first reaction surprised her mother: "Are you suggesting that we have problems?" she snapped. "Bob and I have always been happy. Besides, I don't think it's really any of your business—and it *certainly* isn't any business of the church!" Elaine's mother was hurt. She hadn't suggested it to criticize Elaine. Well, maybe it was a class for "problem families" after all, and Elaine was right—hers wasn't a "problem family."

But Elaine heard about the class again. Her friend Nora was really interested in it—and a little disappointed. A single parent, Nora really liked to join with other parents; it gave her two boys a chance to be with other adults, particularly with "father figures" (she sometimes worried about the boys missing that). She also liked the opportunity to check out parenting ideas with other parents. With no second parent to share decisions, she sometimes wondered if she was doing the right thing. And she really liked to spend more time with adults, especially if it meant not having to leave the boys home alone. But this class was for "families," not for single parents. Once again she wouldn't fit, she thought. Oh, they had mentioned that she was welcome, but her experience was that family topics were always uncomfortable for singles.

Nora shared this with Elaine. At least Elaine and her family could go. Although jealous and wanting to join in, Nora could at least hear about the class if Elaine went. She was certain that Elaine, with her family at "just the right age," would want to attend. Carol and her family were interested, but their children were mostly out of high school already; it wouldn't work for them, they said. Ann and Ted said they might go if their children were older than preschoolers. Elaine's family was just the right age.

Elaine did start to get interested. From what Nora said, this wasn't just for "problem families." Maybe it would be a chance to get Bob to do a few things with the family. Maybe, for a change, they could get Elly into the family for something. At least she could check it out, she thought. Mom would maybe take care of Robby; she really seemed to want us to attend. And that would give Elly and Steve a chance for time just to be with us, without Robby hanging around. He was at such an impossible age!

She was surprised to learn that the class was for whole families. This meant that Robby would have to come. That would make it impossible! It would be more of a headache for her than it was worth. Others were bringing six-year-olds, even five-year-olds, she was told. Well, maybe she could try.

What was the class about? "Understanding Us"? What did that mean? From what she could determine, the class seemed to be about doing things together as a family and maybe understanding more about how her family operated. The posters said it was "fun," "creative"—a "chance to play and to learn together." That didn't sound too painful. She certainly would like to understand more about *her* family! Lately she hardly understood anything that was going on—surely not Elly or Robby—and Bob might understand her better if he had this chance. She could at least ask the rest of the family.

"That's a good idea," Bob said when he heard about the class. "It's about time the church helped some of those families. . . . Us? . . . No, I don't have time to go. The rest of you can go if you really think you need it or want to. But there is no way I can take off a whole evening like that." Later he admitted to Elaine that he really didn't want to talk about his family in front of other people, and it could be embarrassing if they didn't agree on something in public. He didn't like talking about things like that. Elaine told him that she didn't think it was like that from what she had heard, but she doubted that he'd go.

From the beginning, Elly wanted nothing to do with it. "Dumb!" she said. "I'm not going to go to some stupid 'family night' when I could be with my friends!" It's hard to force Elly into anything she thinks is "dumb." If going means we have to come as a whole family, we'll never get Elly there!

Robby saw the posters and heard that it was "building" and "playing" and "games." He wanted to go—"and take Grandma. She likes fun." Grandma is part of our family; she could come—but Grandma didn't think so. She did consider herself part of the family, but "I belong with my older friends," she said wistfully, really longing to get in with younger people and children now and then.

Steve didn't pay much attention to all the talk of a family course. It was OK with him, but they needed to know that he wouldn't skip soccer practice.

They never got to the class—nor did Nora, Ann and Ted, or Carol. Others went—not a lot, but a few. Those who went talked and laughed about it as if they had had fun. It was fun, and they had really learned a lot. It surprised them that the time had gone so fast and that their teens really enjoyed it. Single parent families more than "fit in," and grandmothers were more than welcomed. No one "looked bad." In fact, most of the families enjoyed discovering that they were quite normal. Some things they learned were already helpful. There was talk of doing something like this again soon. Elaine and Bob noticed that some families found new friends and were doing some fun things together since the course ended. Maybe they should have gone.

How will families react when we introduce new ideas and activities about "family life"?

Bob and Elaine are not untypical. Their marriage is fairly normal. One can see that there are untouched problems between the two and in their family system, but they are relatively "well." We would hope that they would attend a family enrichment or education series, but their response is typical.

Many families may not even notice the church's concern about the family or pay much attention to programs and activities that are offered. They might avoid really getting to know anyone at church and end up not involving themselves at all. Men like Bob might shy away from talk about their families or leave "family time" to the wife and kids. Many are too busy to get involved or simply don't like "play" and especially avoid things that might get into "feelings" or "relationships." Families like Bob and Elaine's are busy; work, classes, and children's school activities fill every hour. It is hard to set aside an evening or a weekend even if they say they are interested.

Women sometimes voice a need for time alone or time with other adults—certainly not more time with family—and drop the idea from the start. But women also often show more interest in family things but have a difficult time getting the rest of the family involved. Those working outside the home may limit outside activities simply because of scarce time and energy. To even consider a whole evening seems unthinkable; it could lead to utter exhaustion. But they may also voice a desire for less "task" and more "family time."

Most teens express rebellion at any suggestion of "family time." It is downright embarrassing to explain to one's peers, and besides it's "boring." Most teens can only be persuaded if other teens are also present. If confirmation class members and their families are expected to be a part of an event, they may all show up. Better yet, if a youth group initiates the program, they will likely come in droves. (Surprisingly, once they get there, they may become quite involved!) The topic of the family as an issue or concern, on the other hand, is often of lively interest to teens. Yet, all in all, we can expect that they will drag their feet when it comes to any family event.

Many youth, down to age eight, are involved in other activities that interest them far more. They may like to spend time with the family, but it's certainly more fun to play hockey, soccer, or baseball, watch the Dallas Cowboys, or play an elaborate game of Barbies or Dungeons and Dragons with their friends.

Families with preschoolers are new to parenting and will typically avoid anything labelled "family event." It is too difficult to watch their kids at those affairs, and preschoolers are different from other children anyway. They may feel that family really doesn't happen until they're older. Young mothers' groups and young couples' clubs are interesting, but "family" doesn't interest them. Some may show some interest but feel out of place just yet. It can be helpful to provide some "floating child care" (babysitter available if needed, usually in a nearby room so that the children can participate in activities that they would enjoy) for family programs to encourage this age group to attend.

Single parents will also often avoid family topics or family events. They are just opportunities to be noticed as different. Many are quite interested but would feel that it had nothing to do with them or that separate events for single parents would be better. And many single parents are busy—holding down a job, maintaining home life, and being the sole parent. Few may take the time to get involved.

Families with older children or with children who have already left home often consider themselves to be out of the mainstream of family life. They may not even notice family events. Family ministry may mean helping other younger families—and maybe wishing such things had been available to them when they still had children at home. But most often they assume this is for others.

Grandmothers, grandfathers, and the elderly in particular will set themselves apart and, at best, look on with interest or delight. "Our days of family are past," they will tell you. They will perhaps share some of those days, but few will dare enter as family today.

It seems that all odds are against us. If this is the typical response, why bother to try? It is a typical response, and we've already looked at why we might try.

Most of us have a million reasons why we cannot exercise more frequently, go on a diet, eat better, go back to school, get into vocational training, read more, or take more time for each other. Our response to family ministry is like our hesitancies in any area of our lives. Most of us hesitate to do something about improving ourselves or our situation. I suspect we are creatures of habit and also a bit afraid of growth or discipline. Some things seem to require a lot of effort, and it is hard to change schedules or patterns of habit. New ideas are particularly hard to get into.

I have especially noticed this in working with premarried couples in workshops. Often required to attend, couples come with an obvious desire to be elsewhere—*anywhere* else. Getting ready for a wedding within a matter of weeks or days, couples have a million other things to attend to. Some are even defensive, wondering if our intent is to discourage their wedding altogether. Others, so much in love, see no need to look into their relationship, and those living together assume they know it all already. Yet by the end of the workshop, most share that it was the most important thing they did for their marriage, that they were glad they came, or that they would recommend it to others.

It may be hard to get even a few families or individuals interested in family ministry. And once they are interested, what can they accomplish? Most churches have pretty long traditions of how they operate. If there has never been a particular "family ministry," it's hard to see why they need one now. Negative reactions may be especially high if we suggest bringing in outside resources. And even if we see the need, how can we include a "new ministry"? What will have to change? What will we add? If this means a loss of traditional things or a major rejuggling of what we've had and are used to, it is not likely to happen with ease. For the few who are interested, don't we already have "family night"? Most congregations hold fast to what is and don't relish new ideas or changes.

We can expect these reactions and a strong resistance to change. We will hear a million reasons why each family stays far away from our efforts. There will be stereotyped assumptions that are not true to our new understanding of family; we will have to encourage singles, blended families, and people of all ages to get involved in family ministry. To approach family ministry realistically, we need to expect all of this.

We may also be going against strong forces in our American society. We may be going against the whole life-style of middle-class Americans who find it hard to change their patterns of using their time and energy. We may be fighting the role demands placed on men who see financial support as their key task in the family and on women who may be swamped with domestic and family tasks after a full day on the job. We are certainly going against the peer culture of teens who grant little tolerance or time for family.

Most of us can expect to begin with a few. Even if the process starts in a total congregational setting, a small dedicated core is all we are likely to enlist in the early stages. There is nothing "wrong" with people in their rather typical tendency to hesitate. Much of this is habit. Some of it is inertia or holding onto the status quo (obviously not to be praised but certainly to be understood as quite common to all of us). And some of it comes from what we have known of family ministry in the past. We may never have experienced a holistic and caring church-family ministry. The whole idea of family ministry as we have developed it here may seem strange to some. I doubt that much of this hesitancy is apathy. So let us be tolerant and begin with the few.

Although we begin with only a few, we begin a vision—a vision not just of our own making. I put much stock in Paul's stance that God is indeed at work in every family. We are not in this alone. If our ministry is truly "in Christ," we can change the force of inertia into a flow of momentum. With patience, a few can affect the whole.

With patience, we can afford to accept and honor each one's needs. There is nothing wrong with a young mother wanting time away from her family for a change. We can accept, respect, and respond to that need as well as bring her into fellowship or learning with family. There is nothing wrong with a single parent's desire to share similar experiences with other single parents. One more specialized ministry need not invalidate the whole community ministry. There is nothing wrong with a teen choosing to spend time away from parents; we can also provide this supportive and fun setting.

With patience, we can afford to take time. Particularly, we need to take the time to work with people through some of the steps suggested earlier. Eagerness to rush into something can abort the very thing we most hope for. These step-by-step suggestions do take time. That doesn't mean that nothing with or for families can be done until all of the steps are accomplished. On the contrary, most congregations discover increased interest in the whole area of family ministry when they initiate some family events early in the stages of developing more church-family ministry. Opportunities to come together, play and worship together, and learn more about what it means to live in family usually generate interest in a growing family ministry. But full interest and a more formal program or commitment take time and the careful patience of a step-by-step process.

We also need the patience to listen. Much work and time are needed to extend the vision to all. We need the patience not to project a quick and simple prescription for families, fitting them into slots where we have decided they belong. We need the patience to listen to all—both their interests and their complaints. We need to respect silence, distance, and partial involvement. We need the patience not to set up barricades based on initial response. Keeping doors open invites all to join as each is ready. We must offer doors opening up to community, not leading down narrow hallways. Patience to listen will broaden and enrich our ministry in family.

Once they get into the adventure, most people delight and grow. The postworkshop reactions of those premarried couples are not unusual. Beginning with a few, the families who do participate in learning, support, and enrichment and those who discover family in Christian community will come back for more. When they come back, they usually bring a friend, another family, or some extended family. And so the momentum builds.

How will families respond? Some will respond with eagerness. The growing interest in family ministry within the Christian community was not spun out of a vacuum. Congregations are ripe for this ministry. Laity and clergy alike are asking for resources on the family and exploring the whole area of family life ministry. The church at large is increasing its interest in bringing life enrichment and family ministry into the life and mission of the church. Family ministry is being taken seriously by most Protestant churches at both local and denominational levels. Laity are turning to the church and to church social service agencies for resources for their families. The very sharing of this perspective and these suggestions for family ministry comes out of questions voiced by people in congregations with whom I have worked. By and large, people are interested in family ministry. Most see and feel the need. The question has not been, Why do we need it? The most popular questions asked are, How can we better minister to the family? and, How do we go about doing it?

Most of us will discover a live interest in family ministry. It is hard to uncover that interest until people have something on which to grab hold. Until they see what can be done, they live with what is and may not even voice their concerns. Once they begin to see the possibilities and experience the potential, they open all their hidden concerns and interests. That may be why it is so particularly important to explore this ministry in community rather than in isolation or with only a small task force. In finding out what people need and think, we may discover a real eagerness for ministry. We may even discover an eagerness on the part of particular families to get involved. And there is certainly some eagerness if not urgency on the part of many clergy who see tremendous need and potential within the congregations they serve and call family.

It is with some ambivalence, then, that families may respond—with hesitancy, reserve, and noninvolvement; with curiosity, testing, and even criticism; and with interest, excitement, and eagerness. We need to know this as we enter this ministry. With our feet on the ground, we need to trust that God is at work in our growing care for each other.

Will the response vary between urban and rural congregations? One of the first assumptions I ran across in working with local congregations in family ministry was that rural congregations steeped in tradition would surely show no interest in new modes of family ministry. We were wrong in this assumption. Some of the most solid interest and activity was found in rural congregations. Already more solid or permanent family communities, rural congregations have been most able to further develop church-family ministry in large numbers. Even rural congregations with high percentages of elderly members are interested in family. Couples show up in large numbers for marriage enrichment activities. Whole families come together more willingly; division between youth and adult often seems less severe since many youth are used to working with adults daily. The elderly are more easily brought into the family since they are often already actively part of extended families. In spite of solid traditions, rural congregations are interested in growing in ministry to family.

Whether formal development of family ministry succeeds or not in rural congregations has much more to do with scheduling than with interest. Anything scheduled during chore time or in the midst of harvest or planting will fail. Anything demanding late evening hours will be unpopular. Bringing people together for fellowship, support, or learning will only succeed if we take this into account. Again we see the importance of listening to the people and responding to their needs in the full context of their daily reality.

I still chuckle at the reaction my confirmation pastor first received when he scheduled Saturday morning class a half hour later in order to sleep in 30 minutes longer. To dairy farmers this late hour was more than unthinkable! It meant breaking off from midmorning field work, long after morning chores were finished, in order to drive us dutifully to instruction. Now that I have been the wife of a pastor, I well understand the late night hours put in on visitation, committees, and emergency calls that made that extra 30-minute snooze invaluable before facing a basement full of seventh and eighth graders, but the change was unthinkable to farmers.

Confirmation instruction was a long-valued tradition that did not dissolve in the face of a minor change in scheduling, but that same half hour shift at key times of the day can often make or break a new program or interest. Success in family ministry, as in many other programs of the church, is very much a matter of scheduling and sensitivity to the daily and seasonal context of parishioners. This may be especially true for rural congregations.

It would seem that urban congregations with their higher mobility and higher numbers of isolated families would be most eager for increased family ministry. Many urban congregations are neither community nor family parishes. Many find themselves in the midst of a hectic pace and a more rapid change, not to mention social pressure. Surely church-family ministry here is much needed!

Need has never correlated with response. Noting that our congregation needs a better Sunday school program will not guarantee that attendance will increase with the change. Noting that many need individual support and guidance will not guarantee that they will come in for counseling once we have a pastor who is strong in pastoral care. We may see great needs for family ministry in our congregation but have equally great difficulty in bringing people into the realm of supportive family ministry. Urban congregations have parishioners who have no natural family ties to draw them into extended family ministry and parishioners who may be very busy in the community or in jobs that actually keep them out of town much of the time. All of this makes the development of any community family ministry tricky. It is in urban congregations that I have noted the fewest scheduled series for families or couples. But it is in urban congregations that I have also noted the greatest success with support groups and the greatest turnout at parent-teen events. The urban congregation may lack the solidarity of family that can more easily bring people together, but it does not lack interest in family or community relationship.

The success of family ministry within urban congregations also depends on scheduling, but perhaps it depends more on advertising, drawing people in, and one-to-one invitation. Even more than the rural congregation, the urban parish will seldom find a time that works well for all. But ministry can happen in spite of this. The needs vary and so must ministry in programming and activity.

Each congregation has its own character. Any ministry within it will likewise have a character unique to that congregation. This principle is more important to consider than whether a congregation is urban or rural. The success of any local ministry depends less on geography or density of population than it does on working within the context of the people. Interest in the family is alive in both rural and urban parishes. It is mostly a matter of working out how it will be alive in "our congregation" given who and where we are.

There is a difference in response that I regret to note. For years I was acquainted with a woman and her family, active in both church and community, who showed much interest in full family ministry. Over that period of time, I met several of her friends who grew in the same interest. A core of vibrant lay people seemed to keep the dream of explicit ministry to the family alive in their congregation and community. Time and again she shared her frustration at the lack of support—at times even direct resistance—from her parish pastor. She was given reasons for not scheduling activities "just now"; messages to groups or individuals were not relayed; announcements were delayed. The support of her pastor was clearly lacking. Noticeable ministry beyond the few never emerged, and those few found themselves seeking resources and Christian fellowship for the family *outside* their own congregation.

Similarly, I have seen several groups for marriage enrichment and for parent education or enrichment struggle for numbers. Announcements received their due printing, but the pastor never mentioned the scheduled groups. People were not invited by the pastor or personally urged to attend them. The pastor obviously saw no need to be a part of such a group, and many parishioners made the same decision. Because a few lay people worked hard to keep the ministry alive, at least the groups themselves met for the scheduled amount of time. They were few in number, and there was no organized follow-through on the ministry begun. The lack of clergy support certainly had something to do with the difficulty of getting people involved.

In any mode of family ministry, the presence of the pastor or at least his active encouragement has almost invariably led to greater participation and continued growth and interest in family ministry. The active support and involvement of the pastor seems to be an important factor. Clergy need not "run the show" or lead the group—that may, in fact, not bring added success at all. Clergy do need to support this community ministry, however, by working with interested laity and encouraging people on a one-to-one basis to be a part of it. Parishioners look to clergy for guidance in congregational activity and ministry. A look of disinterest or disapproval can discourage anyone from taking it a step further; a nod or a voice of support and approval can encourage action and involvement. This is community, not simply pastoral, ministry. Clergy alone will never be the sole factor in family ministry, but clergy attitude does matter. Perhaps history or a broader survey may prove me wrong, but I suspect that how our families respond may have much to do with how much our pastor is involved and supportive. Unless you have the full support of your clergy, you may find the development of church-family ministry a frustrating and slow struggle.

I have certainly also worked with a few clergy who were excited about family ministry but who could not move a congregation into family programs or activities. This is indeed frustrating, but I worry less about this side of the picture. It is likely that timing or scheduling, not lack of interest, is behind the lack of response. Patience, listening, and perhaps working it out in a slightly different way might reap different results.

It is possible, of course, that the concern or interest is simply not there. If that is the case, no single pastor could bring it about anyway. I doubt that an active ministry to family can evolve from the efforts and interest of only one person. This could be a sign that something quite different is happening in such a congregation, something that we *can* begin to learn and work from. What we might be envisioning may be too foreign to the situation. We must discover and begin from the actual situation and develop a new vision of nurture and care. I find that situation difficult to work with but one that is less to be feared.

The situation within each of our congregations is part of the picture we need in order to develop a ministry to the family. Knowing the patterns, the forces, and the attitudes out there can help us begin with what exists and develop a solidly based ministry rich in potential. Knowing what to expect and facing practical realities, we need not be disheartened by signs of disinterest, hesitancy, or fear. Believing in our ministry, we can tap into the eagerness and need that is also out there.

Eventually, the question will no longer be, How will our families respond? The issue will become, How is each one a part of Christian ministry and community in family—in daily primary units, in extended families by choice or by blood ties, in the church as family, in the family of the community, in the worldwide family of God, and within all of God's creation? When you sense that you as a congregation have truly arrived at this point, you are no longer facing the situation of a few trying to get the others involved. You are now in the midst of family. You are now within the developing family question of what it means to live together "in Christ." As needs change and as people change, the ministry itself evolves—ever flexible, ever questioning, and ever responsive. And that is, indeed, true to family ministry.

10. Conclusion: What of the Future of Family?

What can we say about the future of the family? If current social forces prevail, I fear that fragmentation frames its future. Families in isolation cannot withstand the strain of economic pressure and social demands. What may well happen is the basic disintegration of the family unit in whatever form. To preserve its values and stability, society as community and as government might assume responsibility for wellness—for child care, education, health, and even identity. Daily we read of more statistics and increased concern about unattended children, unattended elderly, and unattended human needs at all ages and all economic levels. This cannot be. It disturbs our natural desire for wellness and family.

If individualism describes the future, perhaps we are headed for a "survival of the fittest." Individualism in its purest form would make the family irrelevant. A few seem to be able to nurture and care for themselves; a few say they need no family, no community, no other human support. Those who are truly strong in themselves, however, discover that they are not alone, not independent, and not the center of the universe. For all to survive we need to recognize our interdependence. But survival is not enough. Mere survival, the emotional drive of individualism, does not insure fullness of life.

Isolation of family units is a form of individualism. Families who build walls around their nuclear unit present the message: "We can or must go it alone. Hands off!" Because individualism as a form of taking responsibility for one's self is so prevalent in America, most of us are hesitant to break this barrier, even in extreme need. In stories of the death of a young woman in our community, her neighbors confessed to knowing that something was wrong for some time. She was well-liked in her neighborhood, and some had hinted that she should seek help or refuge from her abusive live-in boyfriend. Most worried about it but said and did nothing. When she was beaten to death in her home by her boyfriend, it was too late! I have had neighbors in distressful relationships with a spouse or children. I always wonder if it is any of my business. How long does it take for most of us to report known child abuse or neglect or wife-beating? Individualism is a code of American culture that locks families into isolation where help is not available.

If we regard individualism as the future, at best we will merely survive as families. We may survive as economic units; we may survive as educated beings; we may survive as strong and solid stock. But we will miss the potential of "life abundant." We will miss the love and fellowship of others. We will, in fact, be only a family unto ourselves.

Is there a more hopeful future for all of us? The future of the family as the family of God is promising, for we live in a covenant relationship with God and with each other. We are our brother's keeper—and sisters and brothers in Christ. The family as a household unit is a part of this larger family of God. None of us need to be in isolation or despair. The church in its mission to the family can step past the isolating walls of each family unit and counter the fragmentation of current social forces.

Our homes need strengthening; of that there is little doubt. The church has long agreed. Homes will not be strengthened by bolstering individual isolation, however. Nor will they be strengthened by holding forth one ideal model and excluding all others. Strength comes in upbuilding each other in love.

When we nurture each person in our midst through our ministry, we inevitably strengthen households. When I am "down"—depressed, irritated, confused, or ill at ease—my whole family suffers. When I am happy and at peace with myself, I discover that my family too is usually more delighted and delightful. Whether it is mother, son, father, daughter, grandmother, or sibling, my wellness affects my family. Remember, the family is a system. It is no surprise that fast on the heels of unemployment comes child abuse and the battering of wives. The health of any one family member affects the whole family system. In upbuilding each one, we can indeed upbuild our families.

When we intentionally support, educate, and enrich family units in our ministry, we strengthen family in whatever form it exists. It is not so important to decree what ought to be. It is important to strengthen and nurture relationships as they are. In so strengthening, we will find increased nurture, care, forgiveness, grace, and commitment in those households that are indeed "family." Where the family does not exist as a primary caring and nurturing relationship, our care and love there too will heal, transform, and help rebuild.

The church is a part of the future of the family as family of God. Because the church inevitably involves life together in community, we cannot avoid some relationship to that family. We are together with people from birth until death. We know each member of each family in the church throughout a lifetime and at particular times in each one's life-span. Indeed, we are family. And, most certainly, we list family units on our membership roster.

It is to our advantage to upbuild each household listed on that roster. Building families up with the love and active presence of God in caring community will in turn strengthen the whole church—and each serving member in its midst. Thus at the core of our strength as a church is family wellness. And family wellness, in turn, is always in the context of community, particularly the community of faith. We live in familial relationship to others, to the community at large, to all within the universal family of humanity, to all in the family of God. In the New Testament epistles, messages about the primary family are always in or near the context of the larger community of faith. This context is just as important for our families today. Families belong in the community of faith, and family business is community business.

As always, our families need support, education, and enrichment. Much of this is no longer happening in natural networks of family and community. Intentional loving and caring and intentional nurturing in growth and wellness are needed. To live in truth and grace requires this. We can either bemoan the fact that "families are not what they ought to be," or we can be a part of what shapes, strengthens, and nurtures the family. I prefer to be a part of the latter.

In sharing models and visions of church-family ministry with you, I am optimistic about the future of family life in our congregations. I believe that God's will for wellness is at work in each family, even when I cannot imagine how. And I believe that each congregation can be a part of that work. We may have to open our arms to more of the "nontraditional" families. We may have to open our minds to new forms of "family." We may have to open ourselves to knowing more of our brothers and sisters—and our hearts to knowing more of ourselves. And in reawakening a "call" to life in family, we may have to change programs and structures.

It is up to each of us within each of our congregations to discover what family is and can be for us.

The future of family is with God.